CONCRETE POTTERY
AND
GARDEN FURNITURE

BY

RALPH C. DAVISON

ASSISTANT SECRETARY CONCRETE ASSOCIATION
OF AMERICA

WITH 140 ILLUSTRATIONS

NEW YORK

MUNN & CO., Inc., Publishers

1910

English Garden, Showing Balustrades

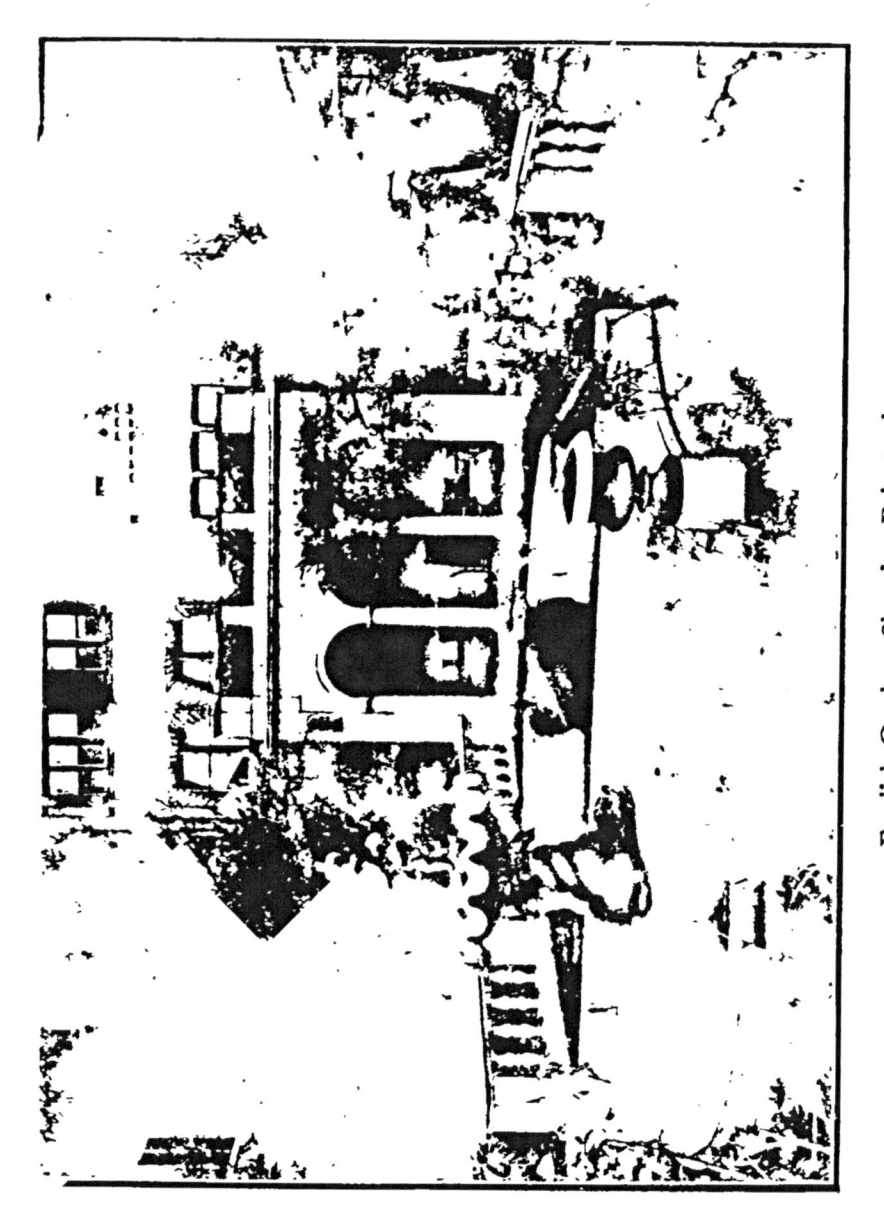

Copyright 1909, by Munn & Co., Inc.

All Rights Reserved.

The right of translation in all languages is reserved including the Scandinavian.

Entered at Stationer's Hall,
London, England, 1909.

192

MACGOWAN & SLIPPER, Printers
30 Beekman St.
New York, U. S. A.

PREFACE

SO MUCH interest has been manifested of late in ornamental concrete, and so little seems to be known about the unlimited possibilities of the artistic treatment of this material, that the author has endeavored in the following chapters to explain in detail how concrete can be made into objects of art.

Numerous inquiries have come to me from craftsmen who are anxious to work in this material but none of whom understand the nature of the material or the method in which it is to be handled.

It is such in particular I had in mind when preparing this work and have therefore been most minute in my descriptions of how the various pieces described are to be made. I have taken for granted that the reader knows nothing whatever about the material and have explained each progressive step in the various operations throughout in detail. These directions I have supplemented with illustrations which I have endeavored to make so clear that no one can misunderstand them.

The method of using wire forms as a base on which to build up the finished piece is original with myself as far as I know, as is also the development of color work in cement. The chapter on the latter as well as those on Garden Furniture should appeal strongly to the professional as well as the layman inasmuch as there is a large and growing demand for this class of work.

The amateur craftsman who has been working in clay will especially appreciate the adaptability of concrete for pottery work inasmuch as it is a cold process throughout, thus doing away with the necessity of kiln firing, which is necessary with the former material.

The textures which can be obtained on articles made of concrete, as described in the chapter on aggregates, in many instances are far superior to those which can be obtained with any other materials, as they have a distinct characteristic of their own and are full of life and sparkle.

Preface

If the reader derives as much pleasure as the author has done in experimenting with the material and in making the various articles described throughout the following pages the purpose of this work will have been accomplished.

RALPH C. DAVISON

CONTENTS

CHAPTER I.
MAKING WIRE FORMS OR FRAMES........ 1

CHAPTER II.
COVERING THE WIRE FRAMES AND MODELING THE CEMENT MORTAR INTO FORM. 10

CHAPTER III.
PLASTER MOLDS FOR SIMPLE FORMS...... 19

CHAPTER IV.
PLASTER MOLDS FOR OBJECTS HAVING CURVED OUTLINES............... 33

CHAPTER V.
COMBINATION OF CASTING AND MODELING—AN EGYPTIAN VASE............ 45

CHAPTER VI.
GLUE MOLDS........................ 59

CHAPTER VII.

COLORED CEMENTS AND METHODS USED FOR PRODUCING DESIGNS WITH SAME.. 89

CHAPTER VIII.

SELECTION OF AGGREGATES............. 99

CHAPTER IX.

WOODEN MOLDS—ORNAMENTAL FLOWER POTS MODELED BY HAND AND INLAID WITH COLORED TILE............... 110

CHAPTER X.

CONCRETE PEDESTALS.................. 122

CHAPTER XI.

CONCRETE BENCHES................... 144

CHAPTER XII.

CONCRETE FENCES.................... 158

CHAPTER XIII.

MISCELLANEOUS 189

INDEX OF ILLUSTRATIONS

	PAGE
Fig. 1—Wire Frames for Cement Pottery	3
Fig. 2—Flower Vases	4
Fig. 3—Pieces of Wire Frame for Round Jar	5
Fig. 4—Bending Wire Lath into Circular Form	6
Fig. 5—Concrete Flower Box	7
Fig. 6—Pieces of Wire Frame for Square Jar	8
Fig. 7—Attaching Rough Coated Jar to Wood Former	12
Fig. 8—Template for Forming Jar	13
Fig. 9—A Good Design for a Plaster Mold	15
Fig. 10—Truing Inner Face of Jar	16
Fig. 11—Truing Inner Face of Bottom of Jar	17
Fig. 12—Wooden Model of Square Box	20
Fig. 13—Window Boxes	21
Fig. 14—Method of Placing Clay	22
Fig. 15—Two Halves of Mold Showing Joggles	24
Fig. 16—Concrete Flower Box	25
Fig. 17—Details of Piece Core	26
Fig. 18—Casting the Plaster Case	28
Fig. 19—Plaster Mold Set Up for Casting Cement	29
Fig. 20—Concrete Jar with Limestone Finish	31
Fig. 21—Correct and Incorrect Methods of Dividing a Mold	33
Fig. 22—Successive Steps in Molding an Outside Plaster Mold	34
Fig. 23—A Core Made in Four Pieces	35
Fig. 24—A Grecian Water Jar	35
Fig. 25—Box for Turning Plaster	36
Fig. 26—Template for Inner Part of Core	36
Fig. 27—A Concrete Vase of Bold Design	38
Fig. 28—Template for Plaster Model	40

Illustrations

		PAGE
Fig. 29	—A Finished Plaster Model	40
Fig. 30	—A Grecian Vase	40
Fig. 31	—Casting Plaster Case	41
Fig. 32	—Plaster Mold in Position to Receive Cement	42
Fig. 33	—Progressive Steps in Making a Mold for a Vase	43
Fig. 34	—Egyptian Vase	45
Fig. 35	—Making Outside Mold and Core	46
Fig. 36	—Detail of Vase	47
Fig. 37	—Assembled Mold for Vase	48
Fig. 38	—Forming Bottom of Vase	50
Fig. 39	—Reversing Cast	51
Fig. 40	—Vases and Pedestal	52
Fig. 41	—Forming Top of Vase	52
Fig. 42	—Mold for Casting Handles	53
Fig. 43	—Concrete Table	54
Fig. 44	—Applying Handles to Jar	56
Fig. 45	—Cast from Glue Mold	60
Fig. 45a	—Glue Mold	61
Fig. 46	—Cast from Glue Mold	62
Fig. 46a	—Glue Mold	63
Fig. 47	—Heavy Undercut Work Cast in Glue Molds	64
Fig. 48	—Model in Position to Cover with Clay	65
Fig. 49	—Model Covered with Clay and Plaster Case	65
Fig. 50	—A Heavy Piece Cast in a Glue Mold	66
Fig. 51	—Model and Plaster Case in Position Ready for Pouring the Glue	67
Fig. 52	—Holding Case to Working Board	67
Fig. 53	—Concrete Fountain	68
Fig. 54	—Concrete Sundial Pedestal or Table Base	69
Fig. 55	—Melting Pots for Glue	70
Fig. 56	—Melting Pot made from two Tin Pails	71
Fig. 57	—Ornamental Figures	72
Fig. 58	—Concrete Vase with Relief Design	73
Fig. 59	—Highly Ornate Concrete Table	74
Fig. 60	—Glue Mold Assembled Ready to Receive Concrete	75
Fig. 61	—Plaster Model of Table Leg	76
Fig. 62	—First Operation in Making a Glue Mold	77

Illustrations xi

	PAGE
Fig. 63—Half of Model Covered with Clay	78
Fig. 64—Plaster Case Being Cast on Model over Clay	79
Fig. 65—Model in Position to have Upper Half Covered with Clay	80
Fig. 66—Model Completely Covered with Clay and Plaster Case	81
Fig. 67—Pouring the Glue Mold	82
Fig. 68—Showing Flexibility of Glue Mold	83
Fig. 69—Concrete Table	85
Fig. 70—Large Vase and Saucer with Design in High Relief	86
Fig. 71—Combination Glue and Wood Core for Vase Work	87
Fig. 72—Copy of an Antique	89
Fig. 73—Vase with Elaborate Color Design	91
Fig. 74—Pompeian Vase	92
Fig. 75—Progressive Steps in Color Inlay Work	93
Fig. 76—A Good Example of Colored Concrete Work	97
Fig. 77—Small Articles of Concrete	98
Fig. 78—Texture Produced with Selected Aggregates	100
Fig. 79—Concrete Urn in White Portland Cement	102
Fig. 80—Flower Box with Antique Stone Finish	104
Figs. 81 and 81a—Concrete Flower Boxes of Selected Aggregates Inlaid with Tile	106-107
Fig. 82—Hand Modeled Vases Inlaid with Moravian Tile	110
Fig. 83—Outside Mold for Flower Pot	111
Fig. 84—Details of Core Box	112
Fig. 85—Mold Assembled	113
Fig. 86—Mold Assembled, Showing Core Box in Place	114
Fig. 87—Separate Pieces of Mold	115
Fig. 88—Method of Removing Solid Core from Cast	116
Fig. 89—Cast of Box after Removing from Mold	117
Fig. 90—Cast of Box after Modeling is Complete	118
Fig. 91—Hand Modeled Vases	119
Fig. 92—Vase of White Marble, Trap Rock and Moravian Tile	120
Fig. 93—Concrete Pedestal	122

Illustrations

		PAGE
Fig. 94	—Dimensions of Pedestal	123
Fig. 95	—Detail of Base Mold	124
Fig. 96	—Parts of Mold Before Assembling	125
Fig. 97	—Detail of Cap Mold	126
Fig. 98	—Detail of Main Part of Shaft Mold	127
Fig. 99	—Shaft Mold Assembled	128
Fig. 100	—Details of Parts "B" and "C" of Shaft Mold	129
Fig. 101	—Pieces of Pedestal Before Assembling	130
Fig. 102	—Assembled Mold for Shaft	131
Fig. 103	—Pedestal with Design in Relief	133
Fig. 104	—Concrete Sundial Pedestal	135
Fig. 105	—Sundial Pedestal.	136
Fig. 106	—Ornate Concrete Pedestal	138
Fig. 107	—Pedestal and Vase	139
Fig. 108	—Pedestal and Vase	140
Fig. 109	—Vase and Pedestal of Bold Design	141
Fig. 110	—A Good Design for a Pedestal and Vase	142
Fig. 111	—Simple Design for a Concrete Garden Bench	144
Fig. 112	—Detail of Bench Pedestal	145
Fig. 113	—Details of Mold	146
Fig. 114	—An Ornate Concrete Bench	147
Fig. 115	—Assembled Mold for Bench Pedestal	149
Fig. 116	—Mold Assembled in Position to Receive Concrete	150
Fig. 117	—Interior of Mold for Bench Pedestal	151
Fig. 118	—Details of Slab for Bench Seat	153
Fig. 119	—Design of Bench Pedestal with Curved Outline	155
Fig. 120	—Ornamental Concrete Bench	157
Fig. 121	—Fence Foundation	158
Fig. 122	—Wood Mold for Fence Post	160
Fig. 123	—Wood Mold for Fence Cap	161
Fig. 124	—Lattice Fence Panel	163
Fig. 125	—Mold for Lattice Fence Panel	164
Fig. 126	—Mold for Coping	165
Fig. 127	—Rubble Panel	167
Fig. 128	—Mold for Solid Wall	169
Fig. 129	—A Low Coping	171
Fig. 130	—Molds, Templates, etc., for Coping	172

Illustrations

	PAGE
Fig. 131—An English Garden	174
Fig. 132—Plaster Mold for Baluster	175
Fig. 133—Plaster Mold for Baluster	176
Fig. 134—Casting a Baluster	177
Fig. 135—Stripping Mold from Baluster	178
Fig. 136—Pointing Up Baluster	179
Fig. 137—Progressive Steps in Making a Baluster Mold	180
Fig. 138—Steel Frame for Fence Work	184
Fig. 139—Making a Cement Mortar Fence	185
Fig. 140—Cement Mortar Fence	186

CHAPTER I.

MAKING WIRE FRAMES OR FORMS

Few people realize that anything of an artistic nature can be made from Portland cement. Most of us are used to looking upon this material as fit only for heavy work, such as foundations for buildings, bridge abutments, piers, etc. It is not remarkable, then, that the layman does not know that cement if used properly can be made to compare more than favorably with ornaments made from other and much more expensive materials; for even those who are in the trade, and working with it every day, know nothing of the wonderful and endless variety of artistic effects which can be produced with Portland cement.

The author for seven years has followed the Portland-cement concrete industry more or less closely, and for the past two years has devoted his entire attention to it. Some time ago he started experimenting with concrete pottery, and the experiments conducted along this line have developed some very interesting and practical results.

The method of making cement pottery is simple when understood; and if the craftsman follows the directions as given in the following chapters, he will find it easy to produce results which are fully worth while. Each step in the operation from the raw materials to the finished product will be explained in detail, including the incorporation of color effects, water-proofing, various surface effects, etc.

Portland-cement mortar has peculiar characteristics of its own. It is unlike clay. Therefore in modeling it has to be worked differently. In modeling clay one can form it into any shape, and it will remain there, for the reason that it is more or less sticky, and the various particles of which it is made up cling or adhere to one another, and thus hold the entire mass together. Portland-cement mortar, of which cement pottery is made, is composed of a mixture of sand or marble dust and pure Portland cement mixed together in various proportions. This mixture is wet down with water, and then by turning over and troweling, is made into a plastic mass called cement mortar. It is next to impossible to model in this material, for the reason that unless it is placed in a mold or a form is used to hold it in shape, while in its plastic state, it will fall down. The first step then in cement pottery work is to make the form.

There are several methods of making forms. One is to make wire frames on which to build up the cement mortar, and another is to make wooden or plaster molds. In the latter method the cement is handled in an entirely different manner from that used for the former. The use of wire forms is the simpler when there are but one or two of the same shape of articles to be made. When a quantity of one kind is to be made it pays well to spend some time in making a wooden or plaster piece mold, as it can be used over and over again, whereas when wire forms are used a new form has to be made for each article, whether of the same shape or not.

The best material for making wire forms is No. 20 Clinton wire lath having about a half-inch mesh. This can be procured at almost any hardware store. When buying it ask for galvanized wire lath, as this is better and easier to work with than the ungalvanized. If not familiar with this

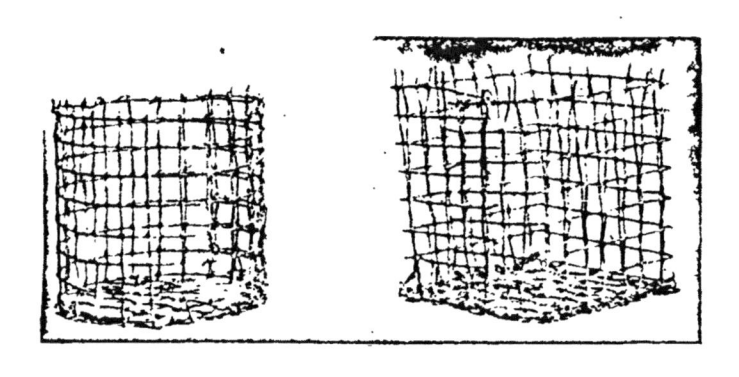

Fig. 1—Round and Square Frames for a Piece of Concrete Pottery

material the accompanying illustrations will give a good idea of what is to be used. The only tool necessary is a good strong pair of tinners' shears for cutting the wire, or better still, a combination wire cutter and nippers, as this will answer for two purposes. In the accompanying half-tone illustration, Fig. 1, are shown two complete frames, one for a square and the other for a round piece of pottery. The latter form is composed of a round piece for the bottom and a long narrow piece for the sides. (See Fig. 3.)

To make a wire form 5 inches in diameter by 4 inches high: First cut a piece of the wire lath large enough on which to lay out a 5-inch circle. Hammer it out until it is perfectly flat, and then place the point of the dividers in the intersection of the wires near the middle of the piece. Set

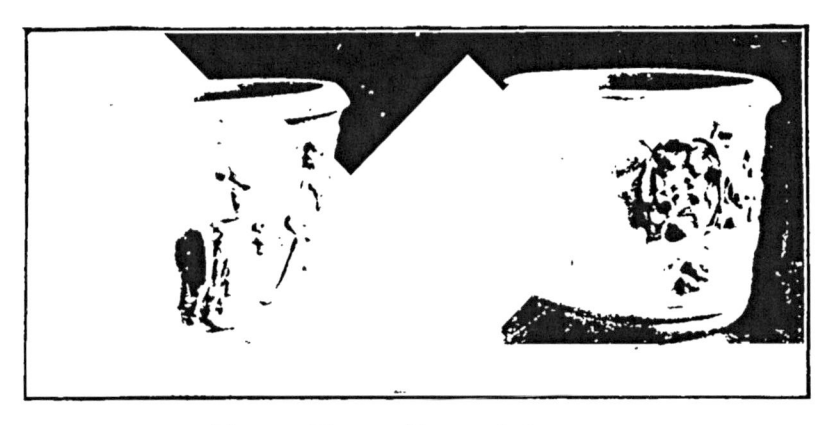

Fig. 2—Flower Vases of Concrete

the dividers to a 2½-inch radius, and scribe the circle. A piece of red or black chalk is best for this purpose, as it will make more distinct marks. Now take the wire cutters and cut the wire directly at the marks, and you will have the bottom of the frame complete.

The diameter of the bottom being 5 inches, the piece necessary for the sides of the frame will have to be three times this length, or 15 inches.

Concrete Pottery and Garden Furniture   5

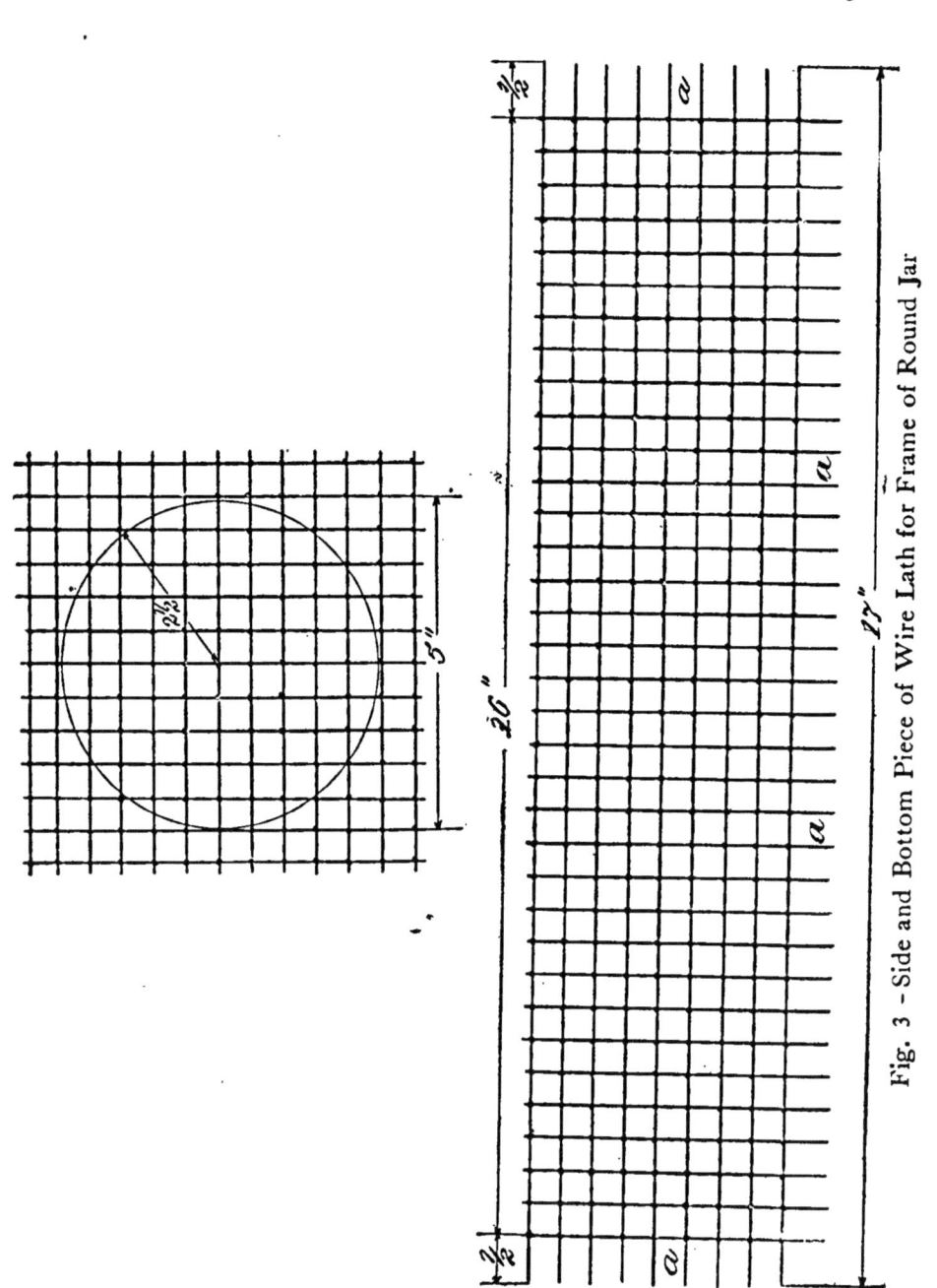

Fig. 3 – Side and Bottom Piece of Wire Lath for Frame of Round Jar

Make it 17 inches long, thus allowing 1 inch for lap, and ½ inch of surplus wire on each end, as indicated at *a—a*. The height of the finished form is to be four inches. Cut the wire lath to 4½ inches, leaving a series of wire strands half

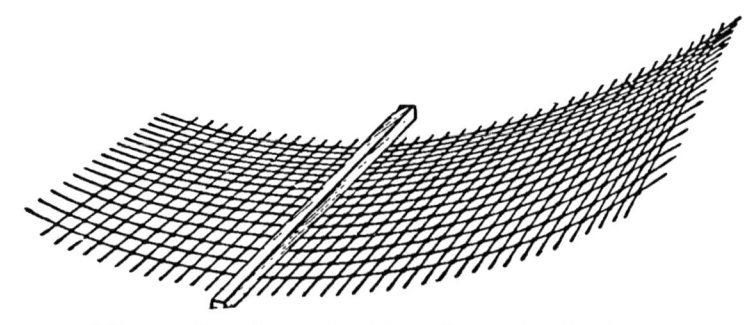

Fig. 4 — Bending Side Piece into Circular Form

an inch long at the bottom as indicated. Now take this piece which has been prepared for the sides and coax it into a circle by placing a straight edge (a piece of wood or metal having straight edges) successively along each of the meshes and pulling up on the free end of the wire lath as indicated in Fig. 4. After the piece is fairly well formed, lap the ends over, thus forming the circle, and secure them firmly to the main body of the sides by turning the free ends of the wire around the strands of the wire mesh, using the nippers to clinch them tightly. After having completed the side the bottom is placed in position, and the half-inch lengths of wire left at the bottom of the sides are used to wrap around the

Concrete Pottery and Garden Furniture 7

bottom and secure it in place. It is not essential to have this frame absolutely round or true, as it is used merely as a surface on which to build up the cement. The cement when once in place can be trued up by methods which will be explained in the next chapter. The square frame which is also illustrated is made in a similar manner. Care

Fig. 5—Concrete Flower Box—Executed by the Erkins Studios

must be taken, however, to get the corner lines perpendicular to the base, for if this is not done it will cause trouble later on when truing up the sides.

In cutting the wire lath for the sides of the rectangular frame, as indicated in Fig. 6, do not forget to make it at least two inches longer than

8   Concrete Pottery and Garden Furniture

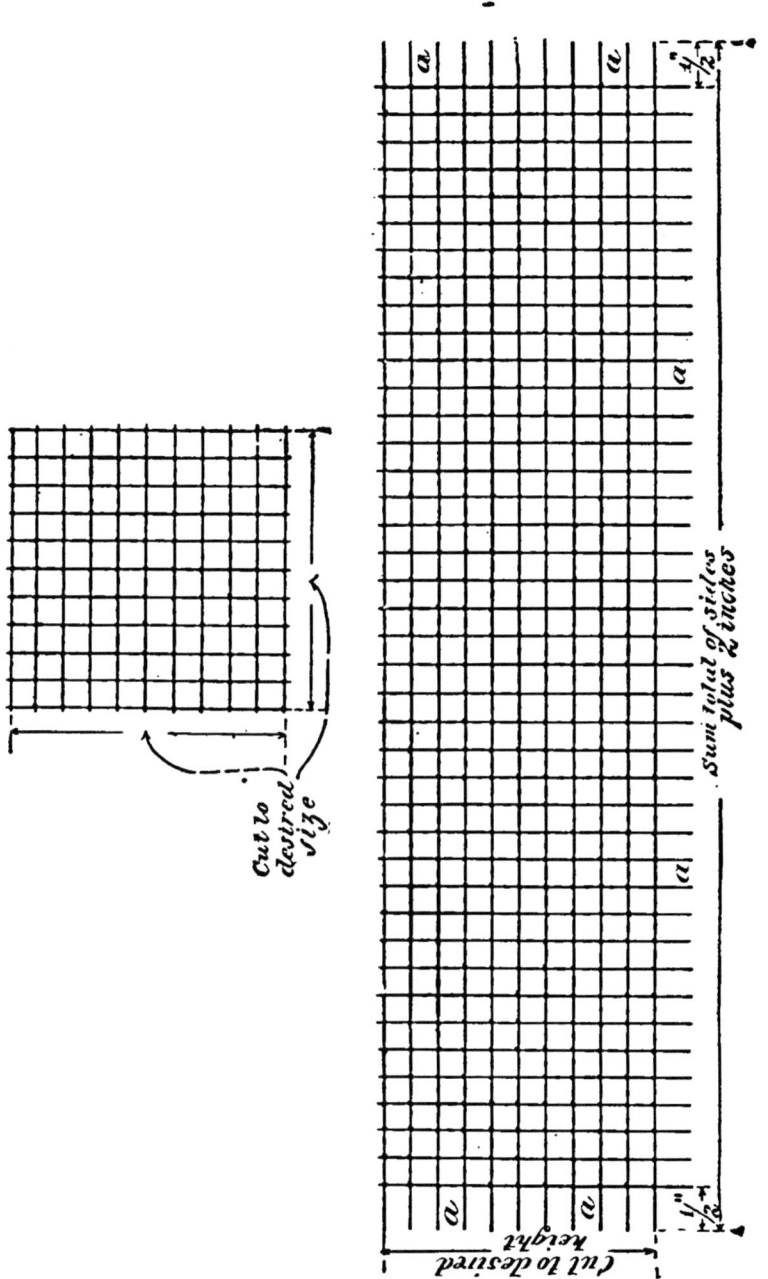

Fig. 6 — Side and Bottom Pieces for Rectangular Jar

the sum total of the four sides. This will allow plenty for the lap and for the wire strands which are to be used for securing the ends in place. Of course, one need not confine himself to round and square forms, as innumerable sizes and shapes of frames can be made up, such as octagons, hexagons, etc., as well as forms for vases with gracefully curved outlines, as shown in the accompanying illustrations.

The next chapter will treat of the method of applying the cement mortar and the forming of the finished pottery.

CHAPTER II.

COVERING THE WIRE FRAMES AND MODELING THE CEMENT INTO FORMS

The next step is the covering of the forms with the cement mortar. The first operation is the application of a roughing or scratch coat. The mortar for the scratch coat should be made of one part Portland cement and two parts of fairly fine, clean sand. This is known as a 1-to-2 mixture. The cement and sand should be thoroughly mixed together while dry, and to this mixture before wetting should be added enough plasterer's hair to bind the particles together. Goat's hair is the best to use. It can be procured at almost any plasterer's or mason supply dealer's. It comes in matted bunches, which should be picked apart and the hair separated before adding to the cement and sand. The whole should then be wet down with water and thoroughly mixed. Be careful not to get the mixture too wet, for if so it will not hang to the forms. The proper consistency is that of a stiff paste. Probably the best tool to apply this mortar to small work is an ordinary table knife; for large work a regular mason's trowel or float may be used. Take as much of the mortar as can conveniently be handled on the end of the knife, and commencing at the bottom of the sides of the frame, force the mortar well in between the meshes of the form. Continue this operation until the entire sides of the frame are covered. Then turn the frame bottom side up, and cover the bottom in like manner. The rougher the surface, the better. Do not do anything to the inside of the frame as yet. After having completely covered the frame as described above, let the mortar set or harden, so that it will be securely cemented to the wire frame. In about four or five hours the mortar will have hardened sufficiently, so that the form can again be handled with safety.

The finishing coat can then be applied. The mortar for the finishing coat can be made of a number of different ingredients, all of which will produce a different result as far as texture and color are concerned. The method of applying the finish coat, however, is the same in all cases. Therefore to start with, we will make the mortar to be used for the finish coat of the following mixture: 1 part of Portland cement and 2 parts of marble dust. This mixture will produce a fairly light surface when dried out, and one which is full of sparkle. It should be mixed to the consistency of a heavy paste as before. The method of applying the finish coat and forming the jar to the desired shape is as follows:

First cut a piece of wood, say ½ inch thick, into a circle having a diameter about ⅜ or ½ inch larger than the greatest diameter of the rough coat, which is already placed in the wire form. Now with a pair of dividers find the approximate center of the bottom of the rough-surfaced concrete frame, and put a small hole through the mortar at this point as well as at another point near the circumference. Take the circular piece of wood and drive a nail through its center, and in turn place this nail in the hole already made in the center of the bottom of the rough-covered form. Now turn the jar over, letting it rest on the circular piece of wood, as shown in Fig. 7, and you will note that the wood projects from 3/16

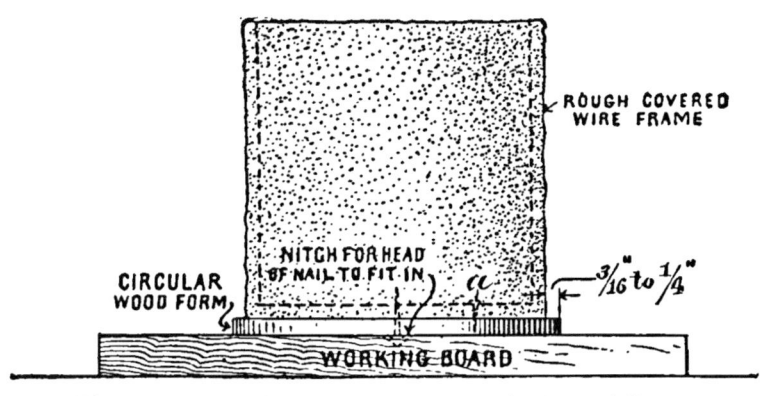

Fig. 7—Method of Attaching Rough-Coated Jar to Circular Wood Form

to 1/4 of an inch all around the rough coat. The finish coat must be built out as far as this. Before going further drive a nail or tack lightly into the wood through the hole which was made in the bottom of the jar near its circumference, as indicated at *a*, Fig. 7. This will hold the jar to the circular wood form, so that it will turn with it. As shown in the illustration, the head of the nail in the center of the circular piece of wood should project beyond the bottom, and a niche should be cut in the working board for it to fit in. The head of the nail will then act as an axis around which the wood and jar can be revolved.

The next step is to make a template or forming strip for the outside of the jar. In this case the jar has perfectly straight sides, therefore all that is necessary is a straight piece of wood. It should be made one inch or more longer than the

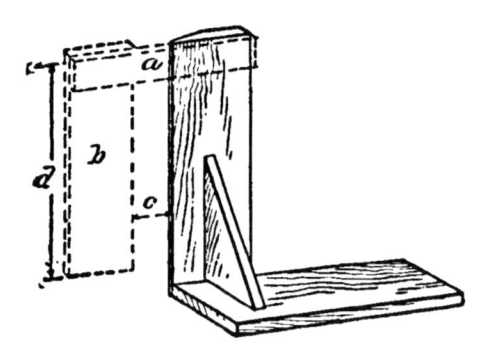

Fig. 8—Former or Template for Truing Outside of Jars

distance from the working board to the top of the finished jar, and should be mounted on a frame, as shown in the illustration, Fig. 8, so that it will be perpendicular at all times. The cutting edge of the forming strip should be beveled off as shown. After making this, all of the tools necessary for the forming of the jar are complete, and the putting on of the finishing coat can be commenced.

This is done as follows: First rough up and

scratch with a sharp tool, such as the teeth of a saw blade, the rough-coated jar, and then thoroughly wash off with a brush and water any loose particles of cement that may be present. Then, as was done in placing the roughing coat, take as much of the already prepared finishing coat as can be held on the end of a knife blade, and commencing at the bottom of the jar build out to the edge of the circular piece of wood which acts as a guide for the forming template.

Cover the whole surface with the finishing coat, gradually building it out to the required thickness. Now hold the template firmly against the circular guide, and at the same time revolve the jar. By so doing, all surplus cement will be cut or scraped off by the edge of the upright template, thus giving a perfectly smooth and true surface to the jar. After this operation it will be found that the top of the sides of the jar are left in rather a crude, rough state. To even these up and to obtain uniform height, nail a piece of wood, as indicated by the dotted lines at *a* in Fig. 8, to the upright template, and at the proper elevation to scrape the top of the sides to the desired level.

Again place the template in position against the edge of the circular wood guide at the bottom of the jar, and start revolving the piece. The projecting piece of wood *a*, which has been attached to the upright template, will strike the high spots and cut them off. Thin down with water the mortar used for the finishing coat until it is a little more of a paste than was used for the sides, and fill in the low spots on top of the jar. Keep revolving the jar and adding mortar until a perfectly smooth, even surface is obtained.

In finishing the inside, the rough surface should

Fig. 9—A Good Design for a Plaster Mould—By Emerson & Norris Co.

be scratched and washed as was the outside surface before starting to lay on the finish coat. Having the outside surface as a guide, it is an easy matter to true up the inside without any further tools than a thin straight edge or a long table knife. But if one feels that he cannot make a true enough surface, another strip of wood, as shown at *b*, Fig. 8, can be attached to piece *a*, which has already been secured to the upright template, in which case the distance c should be the same as the desired thickness of the finished walls of the jar, and the distance d should be the same as the desired inside depth. Then by placing the template or forming tool as shown in Fig. 10 and revolving the jar, a true surface will be obtained. It will be found that the lower end of the strip b while revolving in the jar has formed

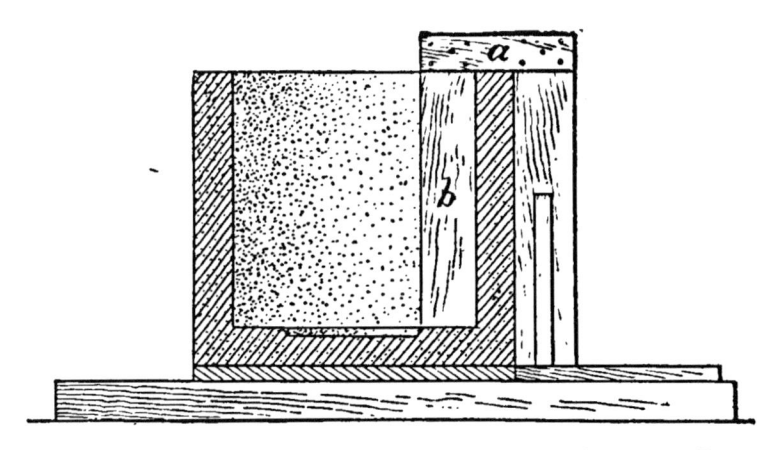

Fig. 10—The Former Arranged for Truing the Inner Face of the Side Wall

a ring at the bottom of the jar, from the surplus cement mortar which has fallen from the sides. This ring acts as an excellent guide for truing up the inner surface of the bottom. If there is not enough surplus cement in the bottom of the jar to true up the center portion of it, add a little more and tamp or tap it down until it appears about even with the ring around the sides. Then take a piece of wood with a straight edge and a trifle smaller than the inside of the jar. Let this rest on the ring at the bottom, as indicated in Fig. 11. Hold the template stationary, and revolve the jar. With a little coaxing and by filling up the low spots as they appear, with a thin mortar, a perfectly smooth surface will be obtained. Having completed the inner face of the bottom,

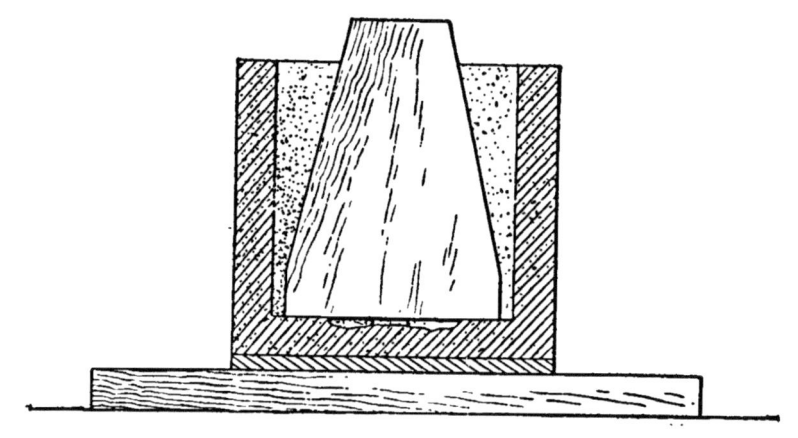

Fig. 11—Truing the Inner Face of the Bottom Wall

turn the jar over and let it rest on its top. Remove the round wood guide which is secured to the bottom by nails, and then scratch the cement surface which is now exposed and wet it down. Now add or lay on the finishing coat, and true it off by means of the same template and former as was used for finishing the top edge, only adjust the strip *a* so that it will allow of the desired thickness of finish to be given to the bottom of the jar.

Now, as far as the finish and form of the jar are concerned, it is complete. Having gone through the operations necessary for the completion of a round jar, it will be easy to build up a square or oblong piece, as the operation is practically the same, the only difference being in the forming and finishing. Here instead of using a round wood guide or form and revolving the piece, a square or oblong guide, as the case may be, is used and the template or former is held against it and moved along, thus cutting off the surplus cement mortar and giving a smooth surface to the sides.

CHAPTER III.

PLASTER MOLDS FOR SIMPLE FORMS

The last two chapters described the method of making individual pieces by means of modeling or building up on wire frames. This is perhaps the quickest and easiest way when there are but few pieces of a kind to be made; but when a number of duplicate pieces of one design are required, it is too slow a method to be used for commercial purposes. Therefore, when a number of duplicate pieces are wanted, it is best to make up a regular mold into which the concrete or Portland cement mortar is poured in a liquid or almost liquid state. These molds are usually made of plaster of Paris. The method of making them of course differs according to the design of the piece to be cast, but when one has mastered the method of making one or two designs, it is easy to make others, for the reason that the general principles are the same throughout.

In all mold work the first thing required is a pattern or model of the piece which is to be produced. If the design is an original one, having relief work, and is to be reproduced from a drawing, the first thing to be done is to model it in clay, and from this clay model the plaster mold is cast.

If the design is simply that of a square or round box devoid of all ornamentation or relief work, the model can be made of wood or any other material. In many instances, it is desired to reproduce articles of a more or less ornate design, which one has already in hand or which one can procure, such as metal or china ornaments, vases, jardinières, etc. In this case, the mold can be

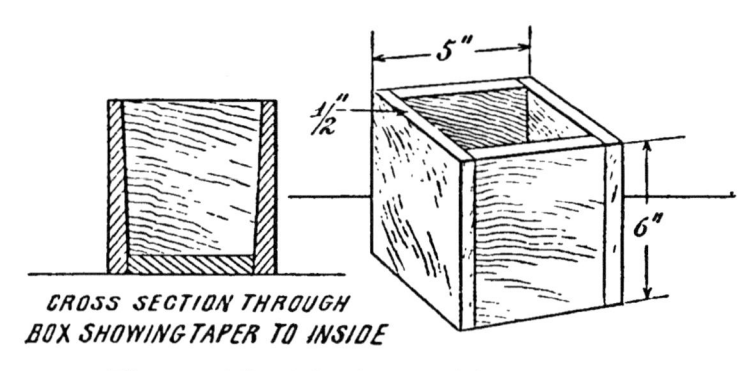

CROSS SECTION THROUGH BOX SHOWING TAPER TO INSIDE

Fig. 12—The Wooden Model of Square Box

made directly from the piece which it is desired to reproduce.

A plaster mold of a simple piece, such as a square pot, can be made according to the following directions: The model for this can be made of wood. The dimensions indicated in Fig. 12 are used merely as an example; any other dimensions can be used, as the piece can be made as large or as small as desired, or it may be made oblong. When the wood model is put together, it should be well shellacked and oiled. Use fairly heavy oil or vaseline. This is done to prevent the plaster from sticking. Now place the model on the working board, which should also be oiled, and

Concrete Pottery and Garden Furniture 21

then take two pieces of modeler's clay and place them on the model at opposite corners, as indi-

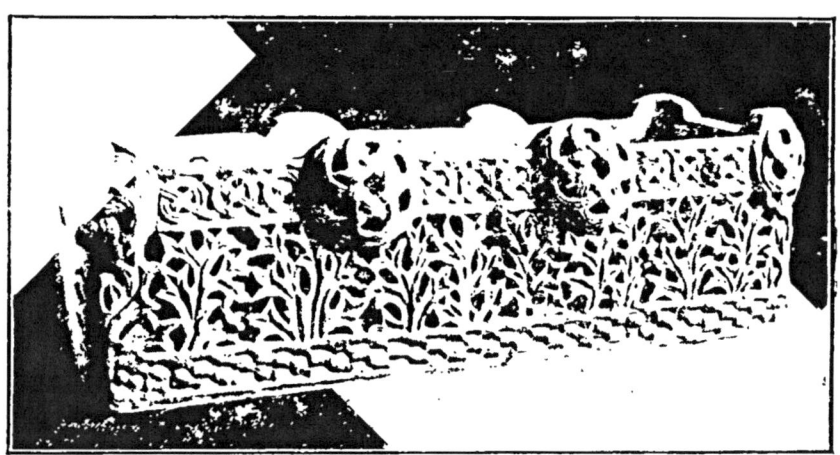

Fig. 13—Window Boxes—By J. C. Kraus

cated at *A* and *B* in Fig. 14. If modeler's clay is not handy or easily obtainable, you can make two strips of wood shaped as indicated at *C,* and lightly tack these in position on the corners in place of the clay. Shellac and oil the faces of these strips. The box is now ready to receive the

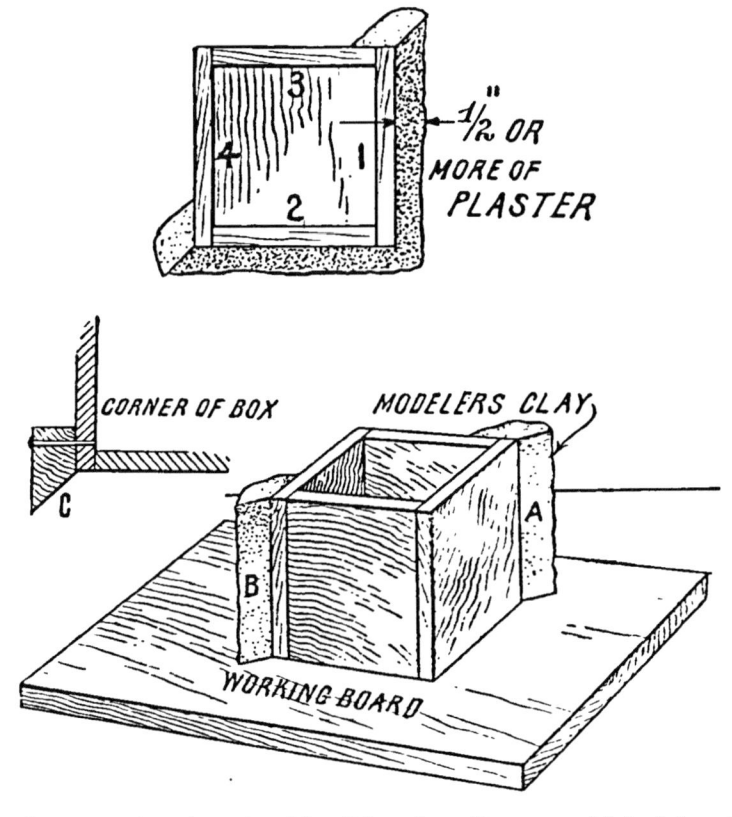

Fig. 14—Showing the Clay Placed at Corners of Model and Plaster Applied

plaster, which should be mixed as follows: Enameled tin or iron ware makes the best thing to mix plaster in, as it is easily cleaned. Place a handful of plaster in your tin, and add plenty of water to it; mix it up until it is of the consistency of a thin paste. Dip your hand into this and scoop the plaster up and throw it on the sides of the model. Cover the sides completely, and keep adding plaster until the sides of the model are covered with at least ¾ inch of plaster; if thicker, no harm will be done. This operation will have to be done quickly, for if not the plaster will set or become hard in the tin before you can use all of it. When it has once set before it is used, it has to be thrown out and another mix made.

The piece will now appear as indicated in the plan view, Fig. 14. Let the plaster which has been deposited on the sides 1 and 2 set for about 10 or 15 minutes, and then remove the strips A and B. Cut holes about ¼ of an inch deep into the plaster on the surfaces formed by the strips A and B. These are called joggle holes, and are provided so that the plaster mold when finished will fit together properly. Shellac and oil the faces of the plaster as well as the sides 3 and 4 of the wood model, and proceed to deposit the plaster on these as was done on the sides 1 and 2. Care must be taken in all of the above operations not to move the model from its original position on the working board. The model and plaster sides should now look as shown in Fig. 15. Before removing the plaster sides level them off to the height of the model. Now lift the whole up from the working board. If care has been taken in oiling all sides of the model, a slight jar will loosen the plaster from it. Then pull apart, as indicated by the arrows, the two plaster sides of the mold.

Lay these aside, and then proceed to make the core or the part of the mold which forms the hole or the inner sides of the box. This is made as

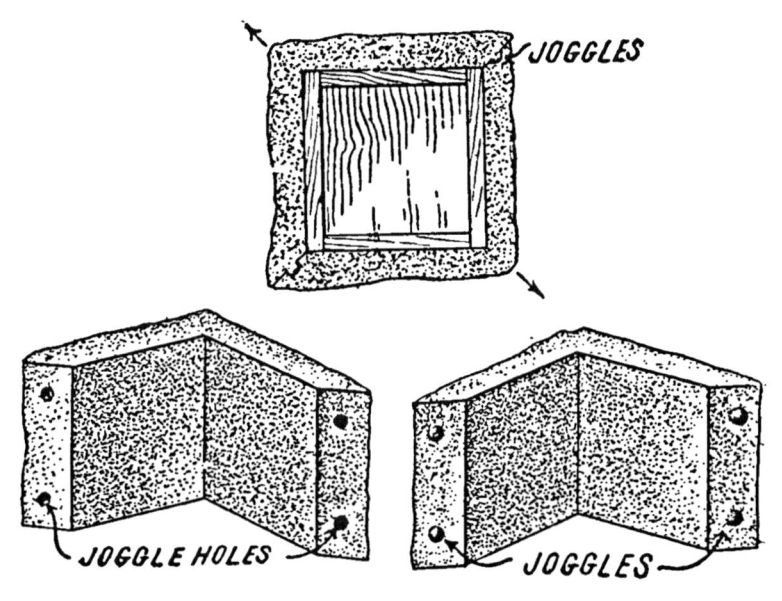

Fig. 15—Plan View of Model, also Two Halves of Mold, Showing Joggles

follows: It will be noticed that in the wood model of the box, which is shown in Fig. 12, a slight taper is given to the inside. This taper is provided so that the core will draw out more freely than if the sides were perfectly straight. Place your model on the working board. Shellac and grease well the inside of the box, and then mix

the plaster as before, and pour it into the inside
of the box. Level the top, and let the plaster set
for 10 or 15 minutes. Now turn the box upside
down and tap it gently. This will loosen the
plaster core, and it will fall out. If the core
should for any reason stick to the sides, the wood
model should be opened a little, so that the core

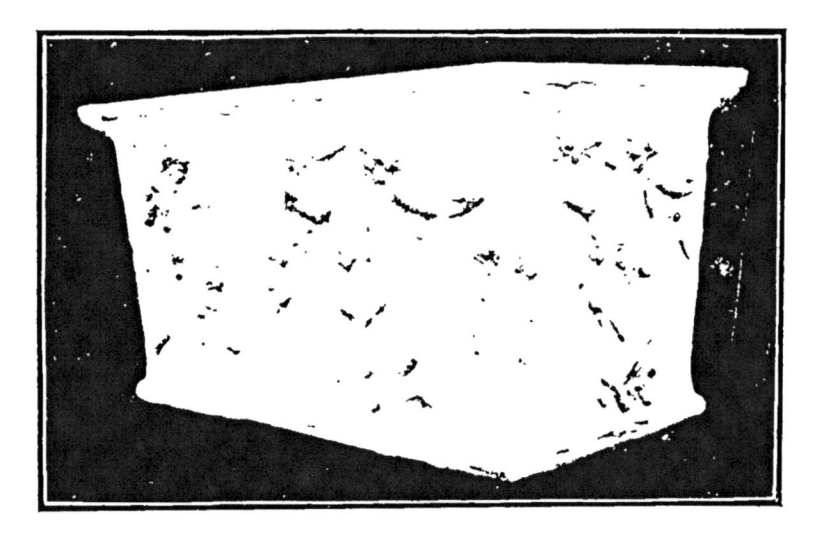

Fig. 16—Concrete Flower Box—Embelished with the "Bacchic
Dance"—Executed by L'Ibal & Co.

can be taken out without injuring it. The core
will then be in one piece, as indicated in Fig. 17.
It should now be smoothed up nicely, and all corners and edges should be made round. Where a
marked taper has been given to the core, it might
be, if well oiled, used solid in the mold when casting the cement.

It is far better, however, to make what is

known as a piece core, as this can be removed more readily, and is less liable to break the cement on removing than is the solid core. To make a piece core, cut the solid core shown in

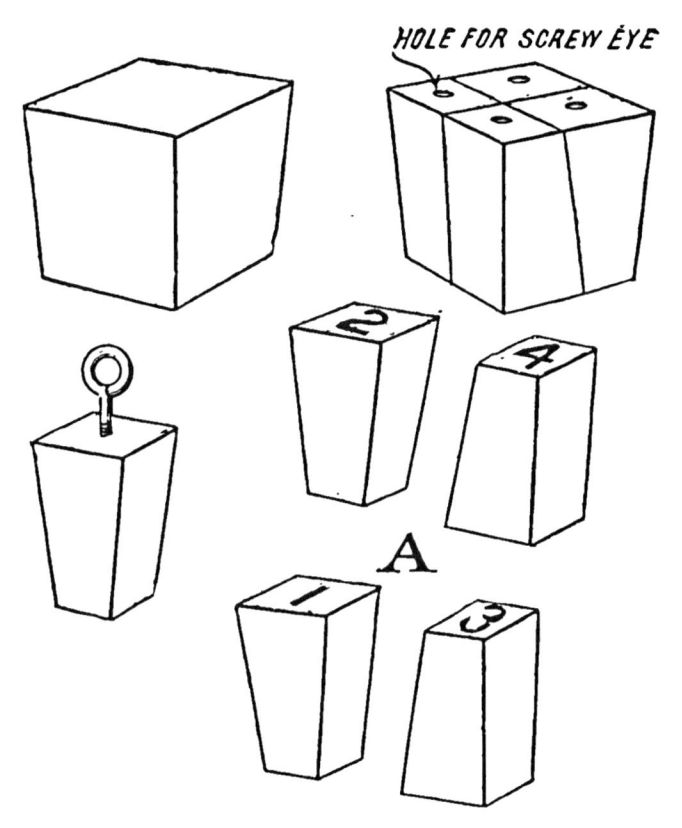

Fig. 17—Details of the Piece Core

Fig. 17 into four parts as indicated at *A* in Fig. 17. This can be done with an ordinary wood saw. If the saw binds or sticks, a little water applied to the blade will obviate the trouble. Mark the pieces thus cut 1, 2, 3, 4, as indicated, care being taken to get the proper numbers on the right pieces, as this is the rotation in which they are to be removed from the cast. Piece number 1, which is a decided wedge in shape, should be taken out first, and it is well to provide in the top of this piece, as well as in the other pieces, a straight round hole in which a screw eye of suitable size can be screwed. By passing a piece of wood through the eye of the screw, the piece can be easily pulled out from the mold.

After having cut the core and fitted it together nicely, as shown in Fig. 17, put it back into the wood model. If necessary, tie a string around the pieces to hold them in place. Also before putting the core into the model, place in the bottom of the model a thin strip of wood; about ⅛ of an inch thick will be thick enough. This will allow the core to project ⅛ of an inch above the sides of the model, as shown in Fig. 18. Taper this ⅛-inch projection of the core as shown, and then place in position, on the outside of the model, the outside plaster molds which have already been made. Tie a string around these to hold them firmly in position.

Now secure by means of brads, or fresh plaster, strips of ½-inch wood around the outside mold, as indicated, about ¼ of an inch from the top. Taper the edges of the plaster mold from the point where the wood is attached to the top as indicated. This can readily be done by cutting the plaster with a knife.

28   *Concrete Pottery and Garden Furniture*

Joggles or holes should be made in the top of the outside plaster mold, as well as in the top of the pieces of the core as indicated. These will help greatly in holding together as well as in assembling the various pieces of the mold. Now secure to the strips by means of tacks a ½-inch

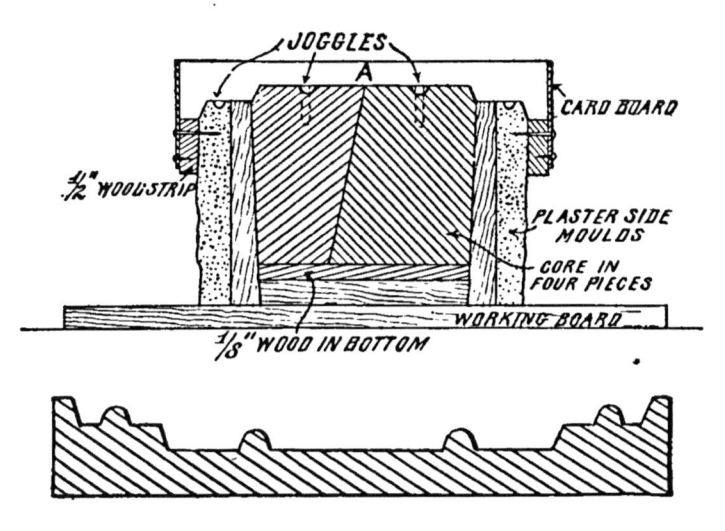

Fig. 18—Parts Assembled for Casting the Plaster Case, also Section of the Plaster Case

strip of heavy cardboard around the entire outside mold. Shellac and oil well the entire inside of the inclosure thus made. Now mix your plaster as before, and pour it over the top of the core, the model, and the top of the outside plaster mold. The cardboard sides and wood strips already attached will prevent the plaster from running down the sides. Smooth the plaster off level with the top of the cardboard, and let it set or harden. When hard turn the whole upside down, and by gently jarring, the piece just cast will come off freely. This piece is called the case. It will have the form shown in section in Fig. 18, and is used as shown in Fig. 19, for setting up

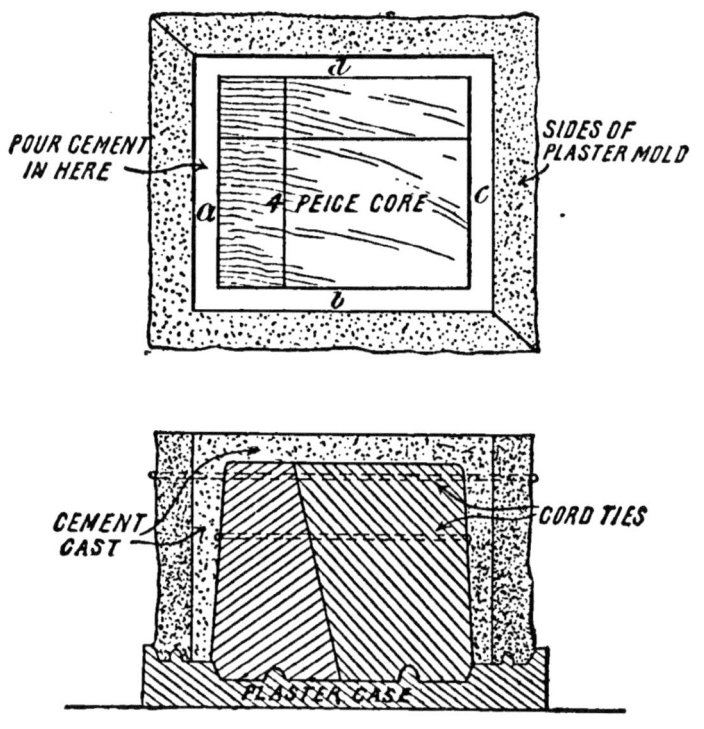

Fig. 19—Plaster Mold Set Up for Casting Cement

the core and outside plaster mold in which to cast the cement box. In fact, it forms part of the mold.

Before casting the cement box it will be well again to shellac and oil all parts of the plaster mold which will come in contact with the cement.

Then set up the mold as shown in Fig. 19, care being taken to bind the outside form firmly together by means of string. The mold is now ready to receive the cement mixture, which should be made as follows: Take 1 part of Portland cement and 2 parts of marble dust, if a fairly light color is desired; if not, 2 parts of any good clean fine sand will do. Mix these thoroughly together while dry, and then add enough water to allow the whole to be mixed to the consistency of a heavy cream. Let it be thin enough so that it will pour freely. Pour this mixture in the openings *a, b, c, d,* between the outer plaster mold and the core, until the mixture is flush with the bottom of the core. Lift the mold and gently jar it. This will tend to settle the cement, and will also force out any air that may be in the mold, and thus avoid the trouble of air bubbles or voids in the finished cast. The cement already deposited in the sides will settle, more or less, under this treatment. Now fill the remaining portion of the mold flush with the top of the outside plaster sides and jar the mold again. Repeat this operation until the cement will settle no more. Wipe off the top of the mold with a straight edge, thus removing any surplus cement, and giving to the bottom of the box a good even surface. Then place the mold in a level position, and allow it to stay there without moving for from 24 hours to 48 hours, the longer the better, as the longer it is allowed to remain, the harder the cement will set. After having set for the above-mentioned time, the piece can be removed from the mold. The method of doing this is as follows: Turn the mold over into the position shown in

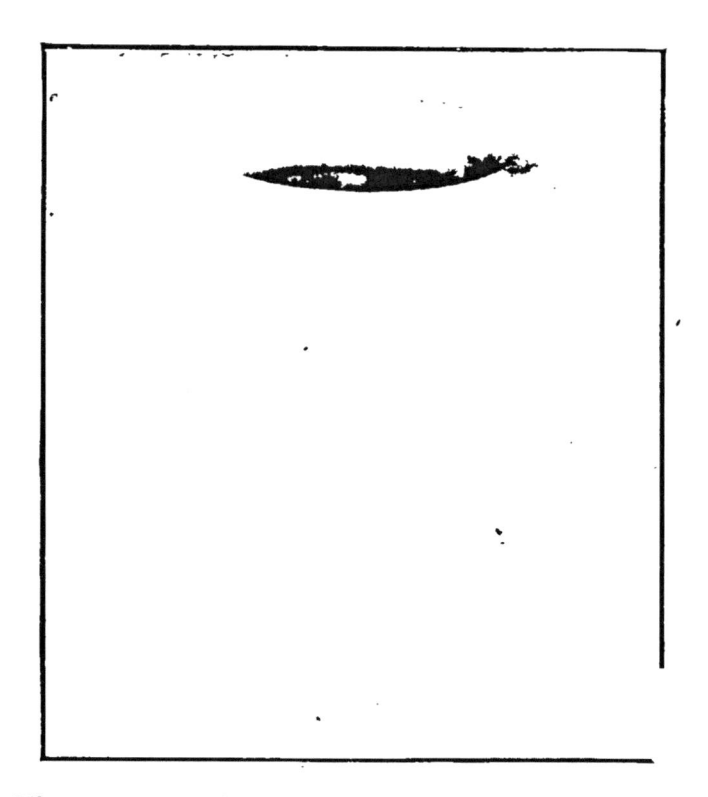

Fig. 20—Large Concrete Jar with Lime Stone Finish—
Executed by Emerson & Norris Co.

Fig. 18; tap the case A around its edges; this will loosen the case, which is then removed. Now take the screw eye and insert it in the hole in the piece 1 of the core. Pull this out, and then repeat the operation in pieces 2, 3, and 4 of the core.

Cut the string which binds the sides together, and then pull them off in the direction indicated by the arrows in Fig. 15.

If care has been taken throughout all of the above operations, the result will be a perfect cast. The next step is the curing of the box. This is a simple operation. All that is necessary is to soak it well with water. This can be done by placing the cast directly in water, and letting it stay there for one or two days, or it can be sprinkled or dashed with water three or four times a day for two or three days in succession or longer; the longer the process is kept up, the better the result. By the application of plenty of water, the product produced will become as hard or harder than stone.

CHAPTER IV.

PLASTER MOLDS FOR OBJECTS HAVING CURVED OUTLINES

The method of making plaster molds for circular objects is somewhat similar to that described for making square or oblong molds in the last chapter. Instead of making the outer mold in two pieces, however, as described for square work, it is always better to make three pieces, as illustrated in Fig. 21, for the reason that in making three pieces the liability of having an undercut or over-

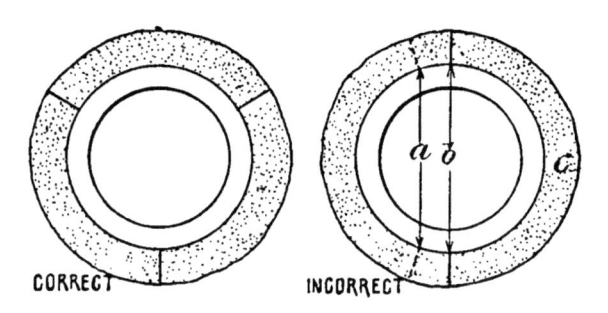

Fig. 21—Correct and Incorrect Methods of Dividing the Outside Mold

hang on one of the halves of the mold is entirely obviated. When two pieces only are made, unless the mold is cut or parted exactly in the middle there will be an undercut on one piece of the mold, which would prevent the mold from freeing itself from the finished cast. By referring to the dotted lines in Fig. 21, the meaning of an undercut will be made clear. The distance a is less than distance *b*, and so the part *c* cannot be removed. The method of making this outer mold is the same as was used for making the outer mold for the square form, excepting that as above stated there are three pieces instead of two to be made.

The position of the modeler's clay and the

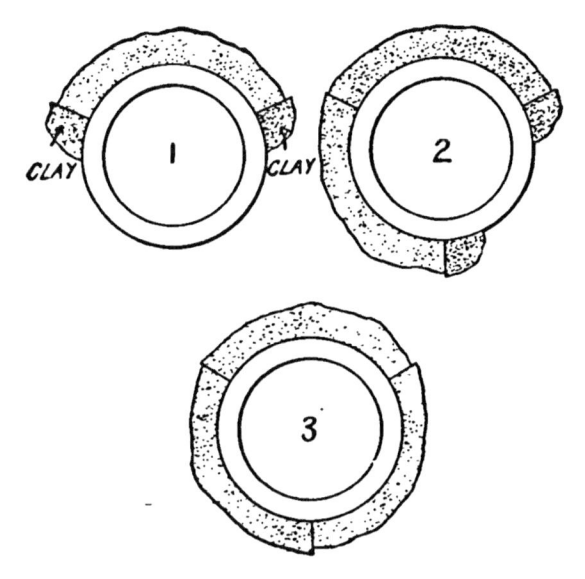

Fig. 22—Successive Steps in Making the Outside Mold

various steps in the construction of the outer mold are clearly shown in Fig. 22. Shellac and oil the edges of each section before casting the next. The sides of the concrete or cement cast, if the object is of any size at all, should be at least one-half inch thick, and therefore the core, which is to be composed of four pieces, as shown in Fig. 23 at *A, B, C, D,* should always be at least one inch

Concrete Pottery and Garden Furniture 35

smaller in diameter than the inside diameter of
the outside mold. The first step toward making

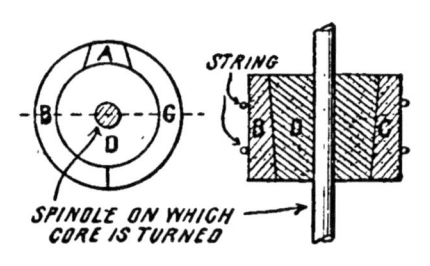

Fig. 23—The Core Made in Four Pieces

the core is to secure a box and fit it up as indicated
in Fig. 25. The tapered center of the core *D*,
shown in Figs. 23 and 26, should be made first.

Fig. 24—Grecian Water Jar—Executed by
the Erkins Studios

The foundation for this can be made by winding
around the spindle in the box shown in Fig. 25

cheese cloth or mosquito netting which has previously been dipped in a thin "mixture" of plaster of Paris. After having prepared the spindle as

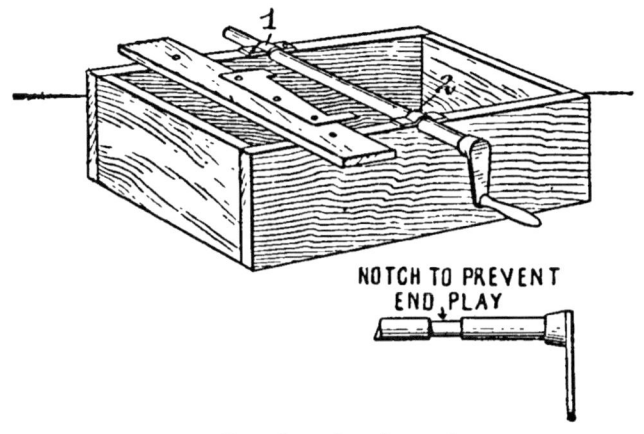

Fig. 25—Box for Turning Plaster

above, a template should be cut from a piece of tin and secured to the box as shown in the plan view, Fig. 26. The tin template should be mount-

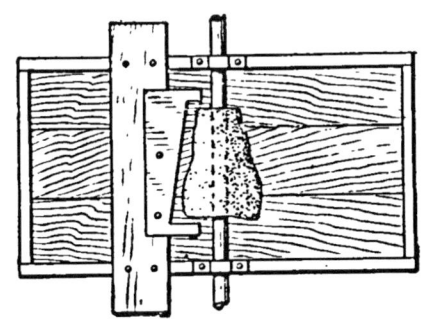

Fig. 26—Template for Inner Part of Core

ed on a piece of wood, to give it strength, and the wood in turn should be secured by small nails in position on the box as shown. This template should be set the proper distance from the center of the spindle, so that on turning the spindle the center of the core produced will be of the exact size and taper desired, as indicated at *D*, Fig. 23.

After having secured the template in the proper position mix up some plaster of Paris, as previously explained, and pour or throw it on the partly built-up core, at the same time turning the spindle by means of the handle. The plaster thus added will adhere to and partly harden on the spindle. Keep adding plaster and turning the spindle until the plaster is built out to the template, which will cut or scrape it off and form it into a perfect cone. To smooth the surface of the cone, cut away all of the plaster that has adhered to the top of the template, and with your hand, which has previously been wet with water, rub the surface of the cone as it is being revolved. Now remove the template and shellac and oil the cone well with either heavy oil, vaseline, or lard.

The next step is to turn up or form the outer portion of the core. A template should be made for this and secured to the box, as was done for the center of the core, care being taken to locate it in the proper position from the center of the spindle, so that the diameter of the outside of the core will correspond to the desired diameter of the inside of the finished piece to be made.

Proceed to pour or throw the plaster mixture on the center of the core, which has already been oiled, and keep turning the spindle until the plaster has been built up and scraped off by the template and the desired form produced to the outer sur-

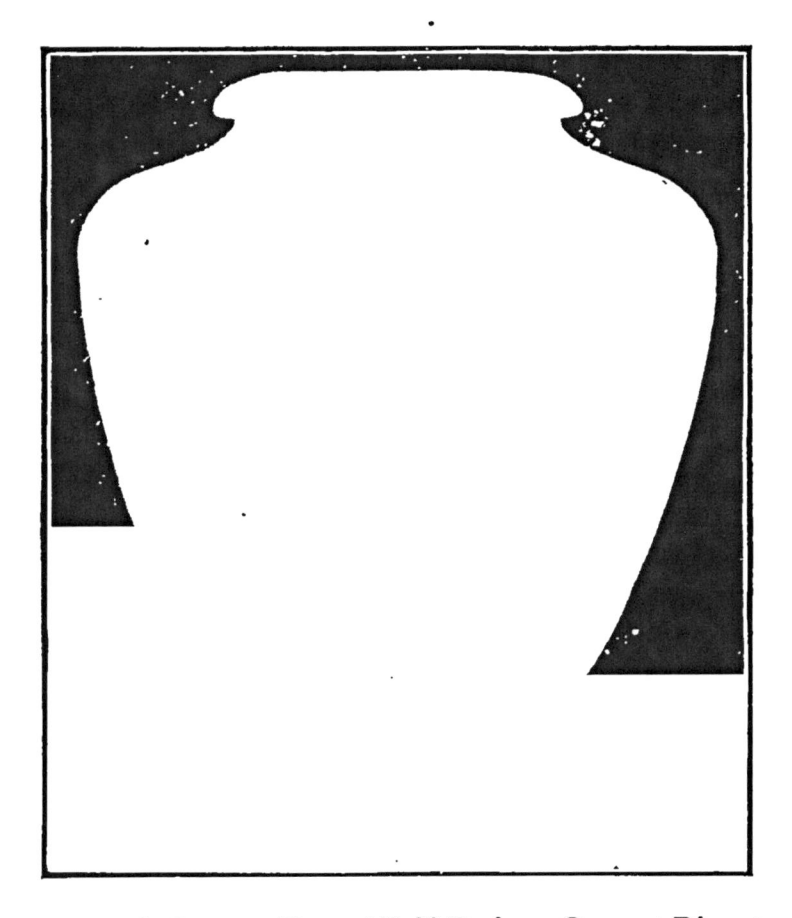

Fig. 27—A Concrete Vase of Bold Design—Greatest Diameter 37 in. Height 42 in.—Executed by L'Ibal & Co.

face of the core. Smooth the surface off, as was done with the inside of the core or cone, and shellac and oil it well.

Now remove the whole from the box by lifting up the tin strips 1 and 2 in Fig. 25, which hold the spindle in place, and part the inner core D from the outer section of the core by jarring the end of the wooden spindle lightly with a hammer. The next step is to cut the outer sections of the core, which is now in the form of a continuous ring, into three pieces. This can be done with an ordinary wood saw; the thinner the blade of the saw, the better. Use water on the saw blade while cutting, as this will prevent it from binding. Be sure to cut the sections as shown in Fig. 23. The section A must be wider on the inner circumference than on the outer, as shown. Now assemble the three pieces, into which the outer section of the cone has been cut, around the inner section of the core D, so that they are again in the same position as shown in Fig. 23, fastening them firmly together with string as indicated.

Then place the core as assembled in the box again, care being taken to get it into the same position as before removing from the box, securing it in place by placing the tin strips 1 and 2 over both ends of the spindle as before. Shellac and oil well the outer portion of the core again and then set in place on the box a tin template mounted on wood and shaped to correspond to the outer section of the finished piece, as indicated in Fig. 28.

As we are now going to make a model in plaster of the finished piece, the sides of which must not be less than one-half inch thick, the template as shown must be placed at least one-half

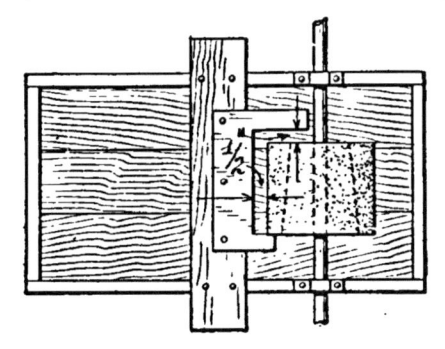

Fig. 28—Template for Plaster Model

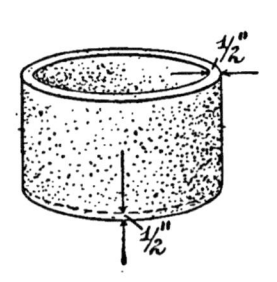

Fig. 29—The Finished Plaster Model

inch from the outer surface of the inner core. After having adjusted the template, proceed to

Fig. 30—Grecian Vase – Executed by the Erkins Studios

throw on the plaster and turn it up until it is built out to the template and shaped into the desired form. Smooth it off with water, and then shellac and oil. Remove the whole from the turning box, tap the end of the wood spindle, and if care has been taken to shellac and oil all of the parts as directed, the center of the core will fall out. To remove the outer part of the core, first take out the smaller piece *A* by forcing it toward the center. The rest of the core will then collapse, and we will have left a plaster model of the box, as shown in Fig. 29, which we are to cast in cement. Oil the outside of this well, and then proceed to

Fig. 31—Parts Assembled for Casting Plaster Case

make the outer plaster mold in three pieces, as already explained and as shown in Fig. 22.

After having made the outer mold, proceed to assemble the parts as shown in Fig. 31, and cast the plaster case, as was described in the last chapter for square objects. Use a clay belt around the outer mold as shown to prevent the plaster from coming down too far. The spindle must be cut flush with bottom of plaster model. Before casting the case be sure to shellac and oil all parts which come in contact with the wet plaster used in casting the case. After having removed the case assemble the parts again, using the case as a base as shown in Fig. 32. Cut the spindle flush with the core. The mold set up in this position is ready to receive the liquid cement mixture, which is poured the same way as already explained in the last chapter.

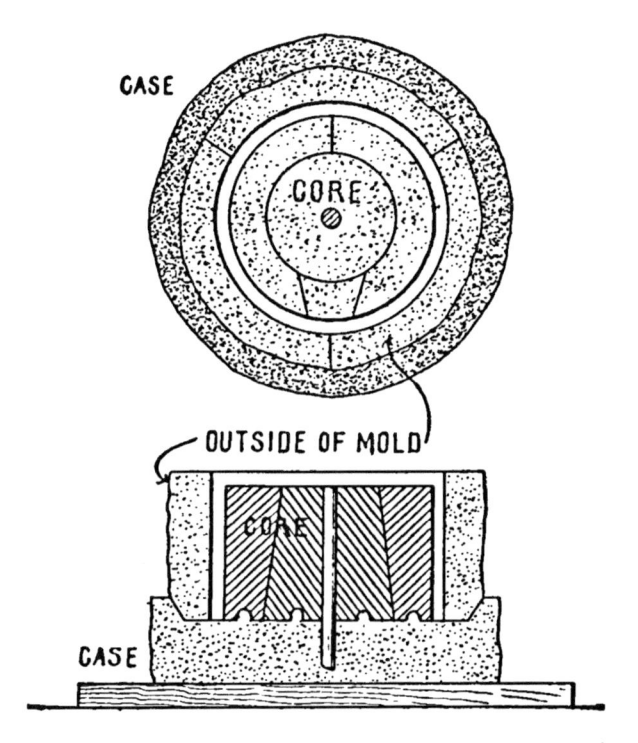

Fig. 32—Plaster Mold ready to Receive Cement Mixture

One need not confine themselves to straight-sided objects, as molds, for pieces embodying curved outlines, etc., can also be made by following the general directions given for the mold just described, the only difference being in the shape of

Concrete Pottery and Garden Furniture 43

the templates used. It will therefore be unnecessary to go into details as to how to make a mold for vases shaped as shown in Figs. 20, 27, and 33, as the illustrations, which show the various steps, will make it clear to one who has followed the previous directions closely. It will be noticed, however, that there is quite an undercut at the point *a* in the vase shown in Fig. 33, owing to

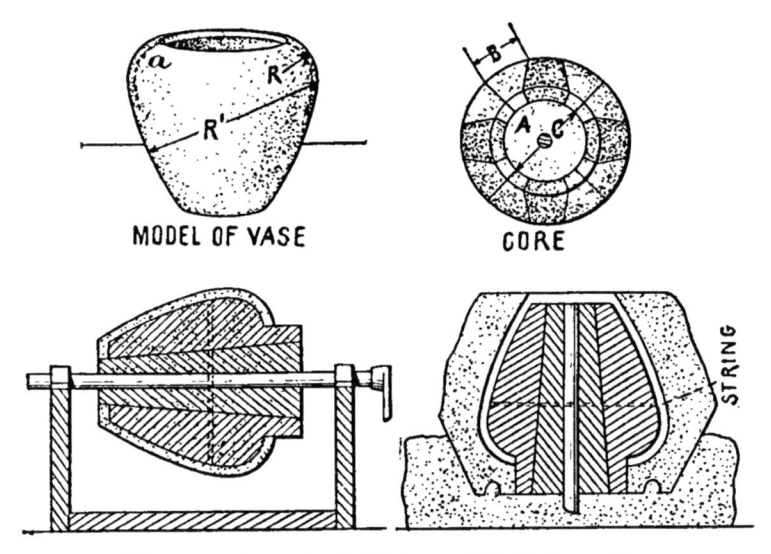

Fig. 33—Steps in Making a Mold for a Vase

the mouth of the vase being of a smaller diameter than the greatest inside diameter of the piece. The main thing to guard against, therefore, in making the mold for this piece is the core. Care must be taken to have the distance B shorter than the diameter of the inside core or cone C. If this is not done, it will be impossible to get the core out of the finished cast. It might be well to state the progressive operations in the making of this mold. They are as follows: First, make inner core or cone. Second, build up outside part of core. Third, remove outside part of core and cut into pieces as shown. Fourth, reassemble core and place in spinning box. Fifth, build up and turn plaster model of piece to be cast. Sixth, remove all pieces from spinning box and cast outside mold. Seventh, cast case.

CHAPTER V.

COMBINATION OF CASTING AND MODELING BY HAND—AN EGYPTIAN VASE

There are but few materials that lend themselves to garden ornaments better than concrete. Like stone, it seems to harmonize with the surroundings and gives a dignified and massive appearance to the whole theme, which is most pleasing to the eye. This is particularly true if good,

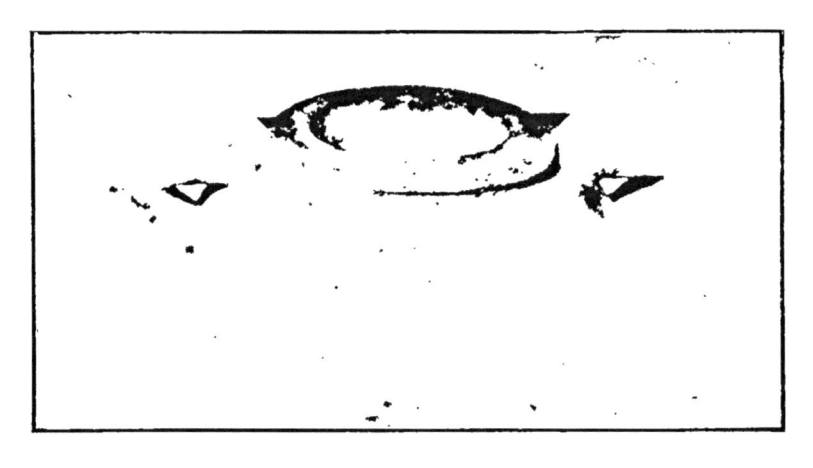

Fig. 34—Egyptian Vase executed in Concrete by the Author

bold, graceful outlines are given to the designs of the ornaments used.

As a usual practice, concrete ornaments are cast in plaster or glue molds. If the piece is at all complicated the making of the mold in which it is to be cast is rather an expensive operation, especially so when there are but one or two pieces of the same design to be made.

The author has designed and made several vases shaped as shown in Fig. 34, which have been much admired. The method used in making them is simple and somewhat novel, inasmuch as it embraces a combination of casting and model-

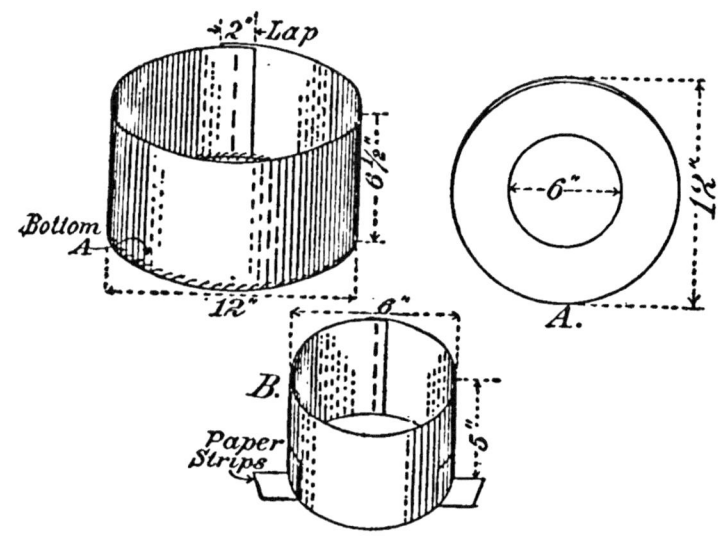

Fig. 35 — Method of Making Outside Mold and Core

ing. A description of how these vases are made may be of interest to those readers who are apt at making things and who wish to beautify their lawns or gardens at a minimum expense.

By closely following the instructions given in the detailed descriptions of the various operations used in the making of the vase illustrated, the

Concrete Pottery and Garden Furniture 47

reader will be able to produce a product equally as good as the one shown.

The first thing to do is to make the outer mold, as shown in Fig. 35. This can be made of heavy cardboard or very thin, pliable wood. In the design shown the greatest diameter is 12 inches, therefore the length of the piece of cardboard to be used for making the outside form must be at least 36 inches long. Make it 38 inches. This

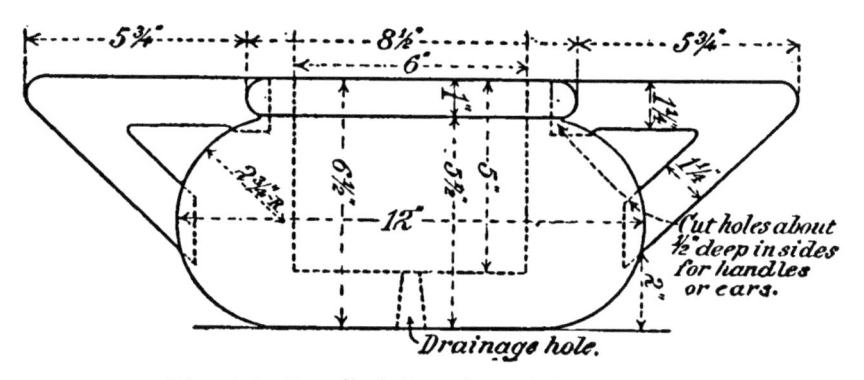

Fig. 36—Detailed Drawing of Cement Vase

will allow a lap of 2 inches, as shown. The height of the vase is 6½ inches, therefore the piece should be 38 inches long by 6½ inches high. Form this into a circle and secure the ends by means of pins or by sewing them together with string. Now cut out a circular piece of cardboard 12 inches in diameter as shown at *A*, Fig. 35; this is to be secured, by sewing, to the bottom of the outside mold, thus forming a circular box 12 inches in diameter by 6½ inches high, as shown in the illustration. The next step is to make the

48   *Concrete Pottery and Garden Furniture*

core, or that part of the mold which forms the inside sides of the vase or the hole. By referring to Fig. 36 it will be seen that the core is 6 inches in diameter by 5 inches deep, therefore the piece of cardboard necessary to form the core must be twenty inches long by 5 inches high. This will allow a lap of 2 inches, the same as was given to the outside part of the mold. Form a circle of this piece, as shown at *B*, and secure the ends in like manner as were those of the outside mold.

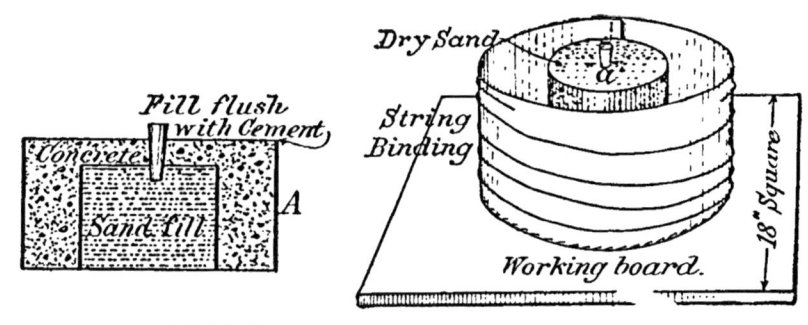

Fig. 37—Mold Assembled Ready to Receive Concı

Now with mucilage or glue secure small strips heavy paper to the bottom of the outside of the core, as shown. Then place the core in the bottom of the round box, as indicated in Fig. 35. Locate it over the 6-inch circle, which has previously been drawn on the inside bottom of the box, as shown at *A*, Fig. 35, and secure it in place by gluing down the small pieces of paper which have already been attached to the outside of the core.

Now fill the inside of the core with dry earth, or, better still, sand. This is done to prevent the core from collapsing when the concrete is placed in the mold. Before placing the concrete the outside mold should also be bound around with heavy twine, as shown in Fig. 37, to prevent it from bulging. Now insert in the sand or earth, in the center of the core, a wooden plug about ¾ inch in diameter, as shown at *a* in Fig. 37. Taper it as shown, and shellac and oil it well so that it will draw out easily from the concrete. Let it project about 2 inches out from the core. This plug will form the drainage-hole in the bottom of the vase. The mold is now complete, but before filling it with concrete it should be placed on a working-board, which should be at least 18 inches square, as shown in Fig. 37. The next step is the preparation of the mixture. In this case, owing to the fact that the piece is to be modeled, no stone should be used. The mixture should be composed of 2 parts of good clean sand, not too coarse, and 1 part of Portland cement. Mix the sand and cement together thoroughly while dry until a good uniform color is obtained throughout. Now add enough water to this so as to make it of the consistency of putty or fairly stiff dough. Work it up well so as to procure a uniform consistency through the whole mass. Now place this mixture, in its plastic state, in the mold, ramming or tamping it down lightly as you place it in. Fill the mold flush with its sides, and level it off as shown at *A* in Fig. 37. Do not disturb the mold, which is now filled with the mixture, for at least

50 *Concrete Pottery and Garden Furniture*

two or three hours. After having set for the above length of time the concrete will be hard enough to allow of the removal of the outer mold, and the sharp corners of the concrete, shown at *A* in Fig. 38, can be roughly cut off by means of a sharp tool such as the edge of a good strong knife or a mason's trowel. The next thing to do is to make a template, or former, with which to model

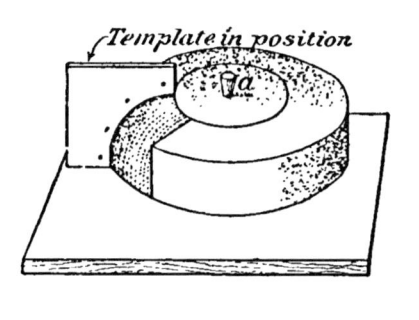

Fig. 38--Method of Forming or Modeling Bottom of Vase

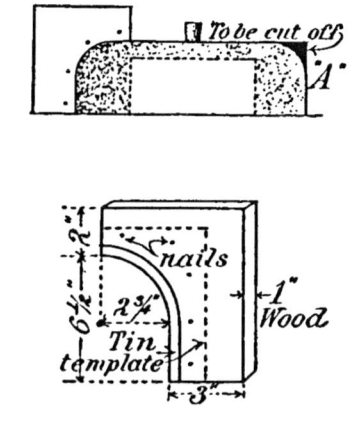

or shape the vase. This is done as follows: First procure a piece of fairly heavy sheet tin or zinc and draw on it an exact outline of the bottom half of the finished vase, as indicated in Fig. 38. Now cut a piece of 1-inch thick wood, as shown, and nail to this the tin template, as indicated. Hold the bottom part of this template firmly to the working-board and against the side of the concrete cast, as shown in Fig. 38, and by gradually working it back and forth around the piece the superfluous cement, which is still in a soft state, will be cut or scraped off of the cast and a good uniform outline will be produced around its entire surface. Now remove the plug *a* by means of gently twisting and pulling. Then place another working-board on top of the cast, as shown in Fig. 39, at *A,* and then lift the piece up, at the same time firmly holding the two working-boards against it, as shown, and reverse the whole into the position indicated by *B* in Fig. 39. Remove

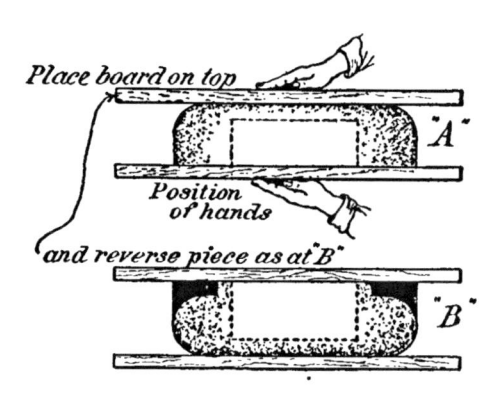

Fig. 39 — Showing Method of Reversing Cast

the board which is now on top, as well as the cardboard disk which formed the bottom of the mold, and proceed to model the upper part of the cast in the same manner as was explained for modeling or forming the bottom of the piece. A detailed drawing of the template to use in modeling the top is shown at *A* in Fig. 41. It will be noticed that the distance from the bottom to the top of this template is 1 inch shorter than the template used for forming the bottom of the vase. This

52   Concrete Pottery and Garden Furniture

is to allow for the depth of the ring around the top of the vase, as shown in Fig. 41. The shaded

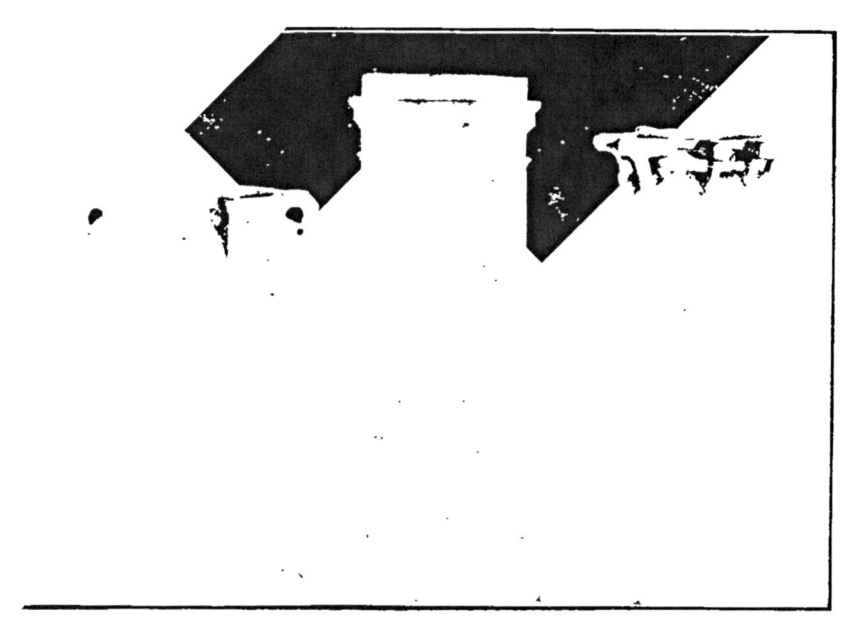

Fig. 40—Concrete Vases and Pedestal - Executed by Emerson & Norris Co.

portion in Fig. 39 represents the superfluous cement which is to be cut away from the top of the cast before starting to use the template to form

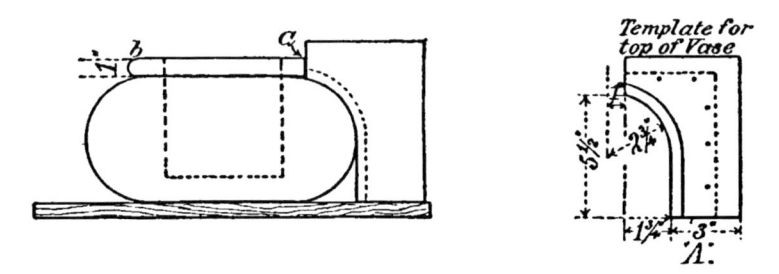

Fig. 41—Method of Forming Top of Vase

the finished outline of the vase. The square edges which will be left on the ring by the template, as indicated at *a* in Fig. 41, can be rounded off by hand, with a pointing tool or knife, as shown at *b*. The body of the vase is now complete, and it can be set aside to harden. Do not

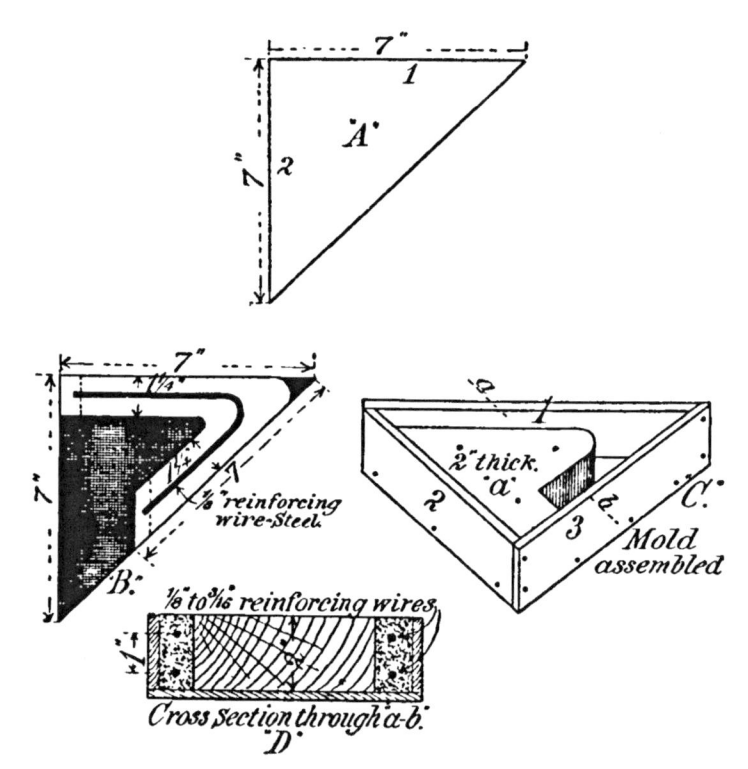

Fig. 42—Mold in which to Cast Handles or Ears

attempt to remove it from the working-board for at least eight to twelve hours, for, as yet, it is in a soft state and must be handled carefully.

The next step is to cast the ears or handles. To do this a model must be made as follows:

First procure a piece of wood and cut it into a triangle, as shown at A in Fig. 42. Make the two sides marked 1 and 2, 7 inches long. Now lay out the outline of the handle on this piece of wood, as shown by the unshaded part at B, closely following the dimensions given. The dotted lines

Fig. 43 - Concrete Table—Executed by
Emerson & Norris Co.

on the two ends of the handle show a projection of about ⅜ inch. This length is added to the handle in order to insert it into niches or holes which are later to be cut in the sides of the vase for this purpose. A piece of wood should now be cut out to conform to the outline of the shaded portion shown in Fig. 42 at B. This should be made of wood 2 inches thick or should be built up of two 1-inch boards, as it forms the inner part of the mold for the handles, which are to be 2 inches wide. Secure this piece, by nails, in position on the triangular piece of wood, as shown at *C* in Fig. 42, and then nail lightly to the outside of the triangle strips of wood as shown. Be sure to have them lap as indicated. The tops of these strips should also be on a level with the top of the solid block *a*, or a distance of 2 inches from the inside bottom of the triangular piece, as shown in the cross-section at *D* in Fig. 42. Shellac and oil the inside of the mold well to prevent the concrete from sticking.

Now secure four pieces of steel wire 1/8 to 3/16 inch in diameter and from 13 inches to 14 inches long, and bend them to the shape shown by the heavy dark line in the plan drawing at *B*, Fig. 42. Lay these to one side and then start to fill the box or mold for the handle with a mixture composed of the same ingredients as was used for the body of the vase. Fill the mold first to a depth of ½ inch and tamp or press the cement down well, and then lay in, in the position indicated, one of the wires. Now lay in 1 inch more of the mixture, and press or tamp it down, and then place in the other wire, and fill the mold flush with the top as shown at *D* in Fig. 42. Trowel it off smooth and let it set for from eight to twelve hours, so that it will harden up well. Then carefully remove the sides of the mold; first removing

56   Concrete Pottery and Garden Furniture

side 3 and then side 1. After having removed these two sides the cast of the handle can be easily removed without fear of breaking it. Clean the mold out well and shellac and oil the insides of it again. Then replace the sides 3 and 1 and proceed to cast the other handle in the same way. After removing the handles from the mold wet them down occasionally so that they will become good and hard.

The next step is to cut holes into the body of the vase into which to insert and cement the handles. The sand or earth core, as well as the cardboard

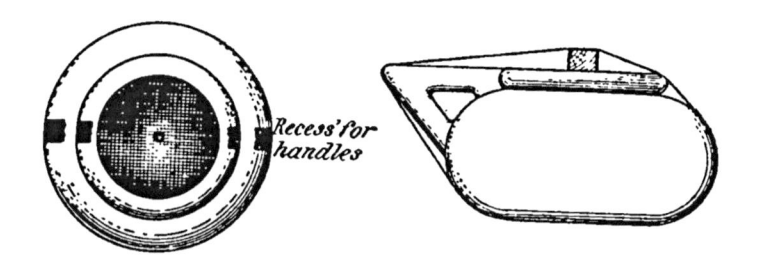

Fig. 44 — Method of Applying Handles or Ears

board lining, should be removed and a line should be drawn across the top and down both sides of the vase at its center, as shown in Fig. 44. This line will show where the handles are to be located. Hold the handle in its proper position against the side of the vase, and with a pencil outline the position and shape of its two ends on the body of the vase. Now with a hammer and chisel gently cut out holes at these points about ½ inch deep, into which to cement the handle. Locate and cut out holes on the opposite side of the vase for the other handle to fit into it in like manner. Now by gently tapping with a hammer roughen up the ends of the handles, and then place both the vase and the handle in water or sprinkle them until they are thoroughly wet. Now mix some pure Portland cement and water together into a fairly thick paste, and trowel it well into the holes prepared for the handle in the body of the vase as well as on to both ends of the handle. Sprinkle both of these surfaces with water and then place the handle in position, firmly pressing it in place. True it up and scrape away the surplus cement, at the same time making a neat finish around the handle where it joins the vase. Hold the handle in position by binding it firmly in place by good stout string. Wedge the string up, as indicated in Fig. 44, to help further tighten it. Wet the joint down well with water occasionally and allow the string to remain in position for at least twelve hours before removing it in order to allow the handle to be firmly cemented in place. Secure the other handle to the vase in like manner, and the vase is now complete.

If by any chance there should be any holes or marked irregularities in the surface of the vase these can be pointed or filled up with a mixture composed of the same ingredients as used in the body of the vase. A good smooth, fairly light finish can be procured by rubbing the whole surface down with coarse emery cloth. Then soak the vase in water and rub over its entire surface a thin coat of a mixture composed of 1 part of marble dust and 1 part of Portland cement. Let this dry out and then again wet down the vase. The oftener the vase is wet the harder it will be. Remember that water is a most important factor in all concrete work. One can never get a good bond between two surfaces if the parts are not thoroughly wet down. The dimensions given in Fig. 36 are merely suggestive. The same general principle and directions as given above can be used for making a vase of almost any size and shape, as well as for making tables, pedestals, etc.

CHAPTER VI.

GLUE MOLDS

Glue molds, or flexible molds as they are often called, are extensively used in casting concrete ornaments in which the design embodies heavy relief work containing more or less undercut. Owing to the flexible nature of these molds, they can be made in fewer pieces than a plaster mold could be made, for the same class of work, and at the same time they can be more easily removed from the cast, while the concrete is still in a more or less unhardened state, with less fear of injuring the more delicate parts of the design.

The only objection to the glue mold is that its life is limited to from five to eight casts at the most, whereas the life of a plaster mold is practically unlimited. In making a glue mold, as in all other cast work, the first thing to do is to procure your original or model of the piece which is to be reproduced. First will be explained how to make a simple one-piece form of glue mold, such as is used in casting pieces similar to those illustrated in Figs. 45, 46 and 47. Take the model of the piece which is to be reproduced, and secure it to the working-board, as shown in the cross-sectional drawing, Fig. 48. A daub of shellac on the back of the model in most cases will hold it in place on the working-board. Now dampen an old

60   *Concrete Pottery and Garden Furniture*

newspaper and lay it over the model. Let it follow the general outlines of the model as closely as you can, as shown by the heavy line in Fig. 48. The next step is to procure some modelers' clay, and with an ordinary rolling pin roll it out into a sheet about ½ inch thick. The model is now to

Fig. 45—Cast from Glue Mold

be completely covered with this sheet clay, as shown in Fig. 49, thus producing an even thickness of ½ inch of clay all over its entire surface. The clay thus placed on the model is next to be entirely covered with a plaster of Paris case of about ½ inch to 1 inch in thickness, according to the size of the piece.

Fig. 45a—Glue Mold

The method of casting a plaster of Paris case is explained in detail in the chapter on Plaster Molds. Before casting the case, however, do not neglect to oil the surface of the clay well, so as to prevent it from adhering to the inside of the plas-

Fig. 46—Cast from Glue Mold

ter case. After the plaster case has hardened mark its outline on the working board, and then carefully lift the case and remove it from the clay covering, then in turn remove the clay covering and paper from the model. If any of the paper should have adhered to the model, clean it off, and then shellac and oil the model well, so as to prevent the glue from sticking to it.

Now take the plaster case and make a good-

Fig. 46a—Glue Mold

sized hole in it at *d,* as indicated in Fig. 51. This hole should be at least ¾ inch in diameter, as it is to receive the end of the funnel through which the glue is to be poured. Also make a number

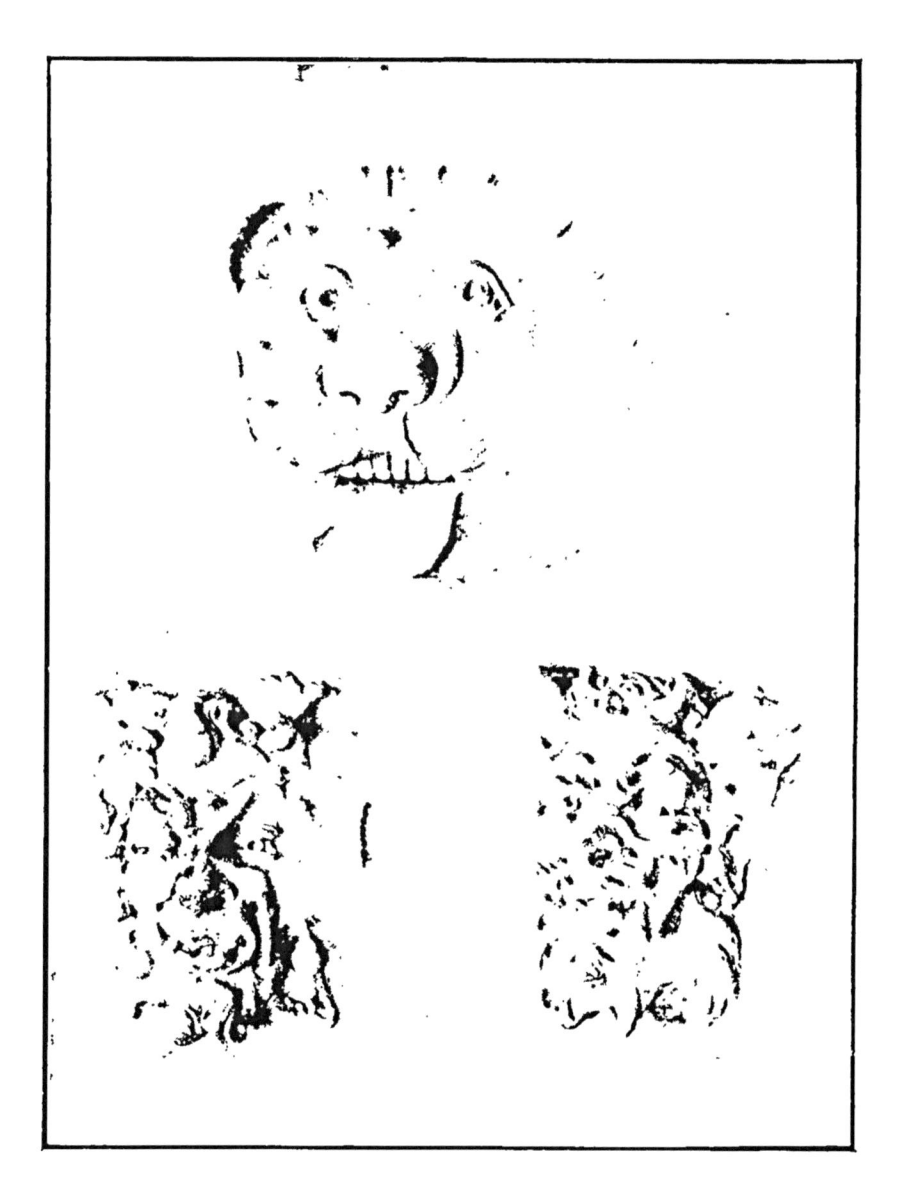

Fig. 47—A Few Specimens of Heavy Undercut Work Cast in Glue Molds

of smaller holes, say ⅛ inch in diameter, at various points throughout the cast, as indicated by the light double lines. These latter holes are

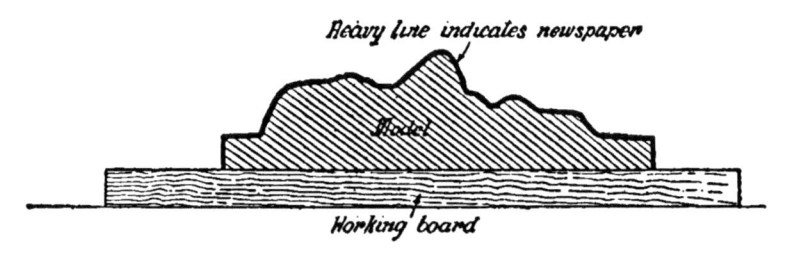

Fig. 48 - Position of Model on Working Board ready to Cover with Clay

vent holes, and are provided in the case so as to let the air escape from within while the liquid glue is being poured. After having prepared the cast as directed, replace it in its original position over the model, as indicated by the outline of it which was made on the working board before it was

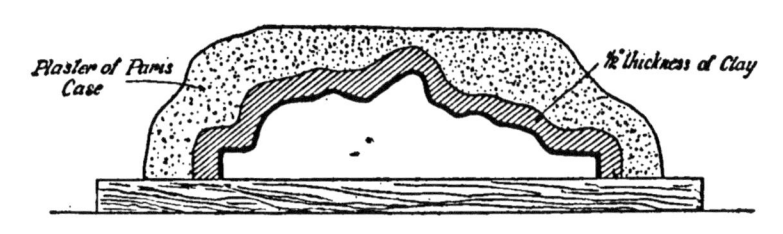

Fig. 49—Model Covered with Clay and Plaster Case

removed from the clay covering over which it was cast. Secure the case firmly to the board by means of passing canvas straps over it, as shown in the end view Fig. 52. Now, instead of having

66 Concrete Pottery and Garden Furniture

an even thickness of clay over the model, we have a cavity of uniform size around the entire model, into which the glue is to be poured. It is essential that the glue should be of a uniform

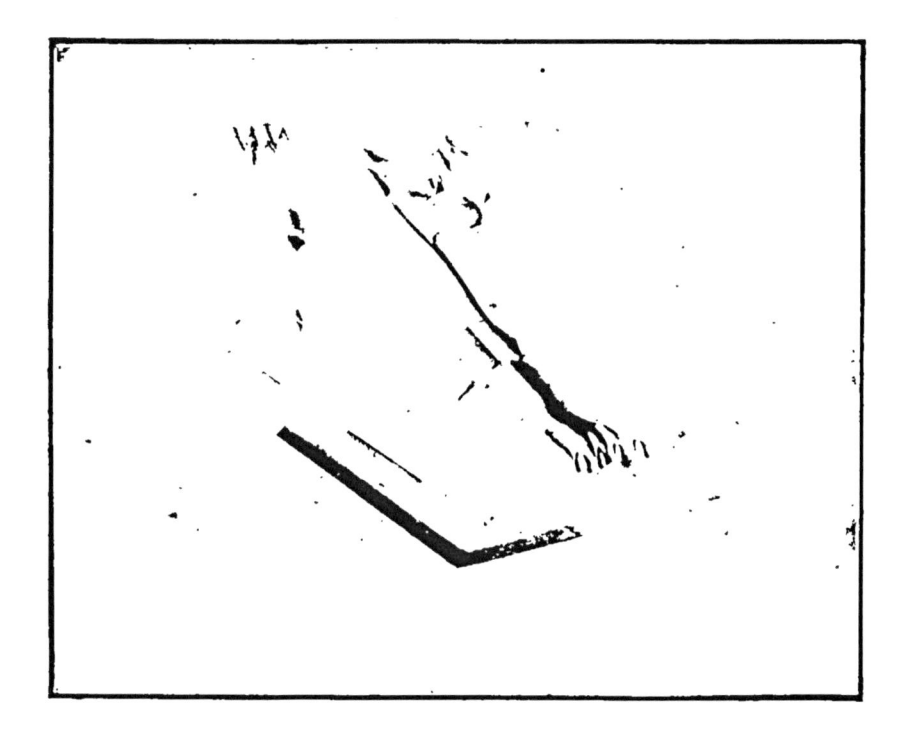

Fig. 50—Heavy Piece Cast in a Glue Mold—By J. C. Kraus

thickness over the entire surface of the model, in order to have it flow properly, and also to produce a uniform flexibility throughout the glue mold. The best glue to use in making glue molds is a fine grade of white glue. This can be procured at almost any paint store. If the dealer does not know exactly what you want, ask for the regular grade of glue of which plasterers make glue molds. Almost any good glue, however, will do; it ranges in price from 18 cents to 25 cents per pound. Sheet gelatine can also be used in

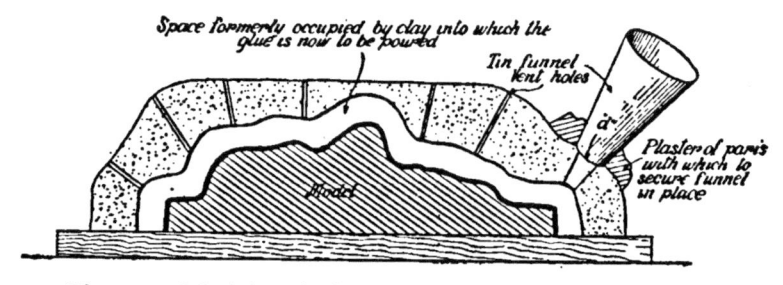

Fig. 51—Model and Plaster Case in Position Ready for Pouring the Glue

making flexible molds, but it is a trifle more expensive than glue. To prepare the glue, soak it in water from ten to fifteen minutes, in which time

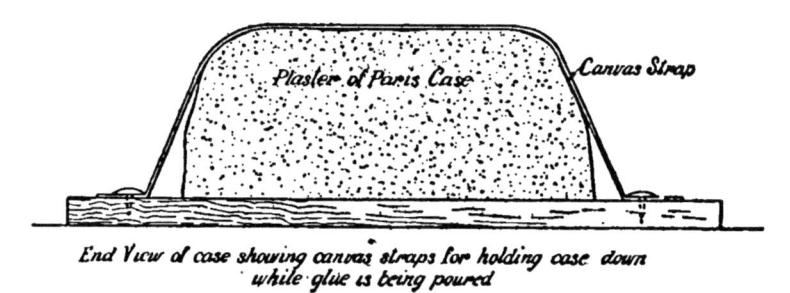

Fig. 52—Method of Holding Case to Working Board while Pouring the Glue

it will absorb the water and swell up. Now take a regular double tin; cover the bottom of the inner tin with water, and then place in it the glue prepared as directed above. If a double tin is

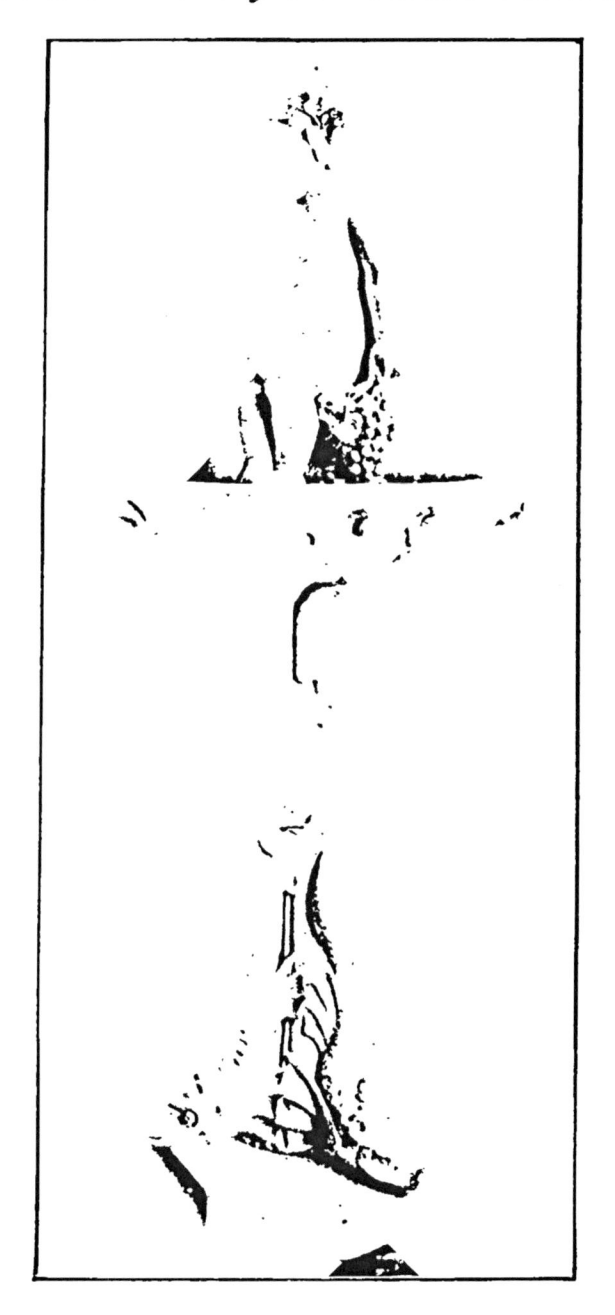

Fig. 53 – Concrete Fountain – By J. C. Kraus

not available, two tin pails can be used, as shown in Figs. 55 and 56. One of these should be placed inside of the other as shown, and the bottom of

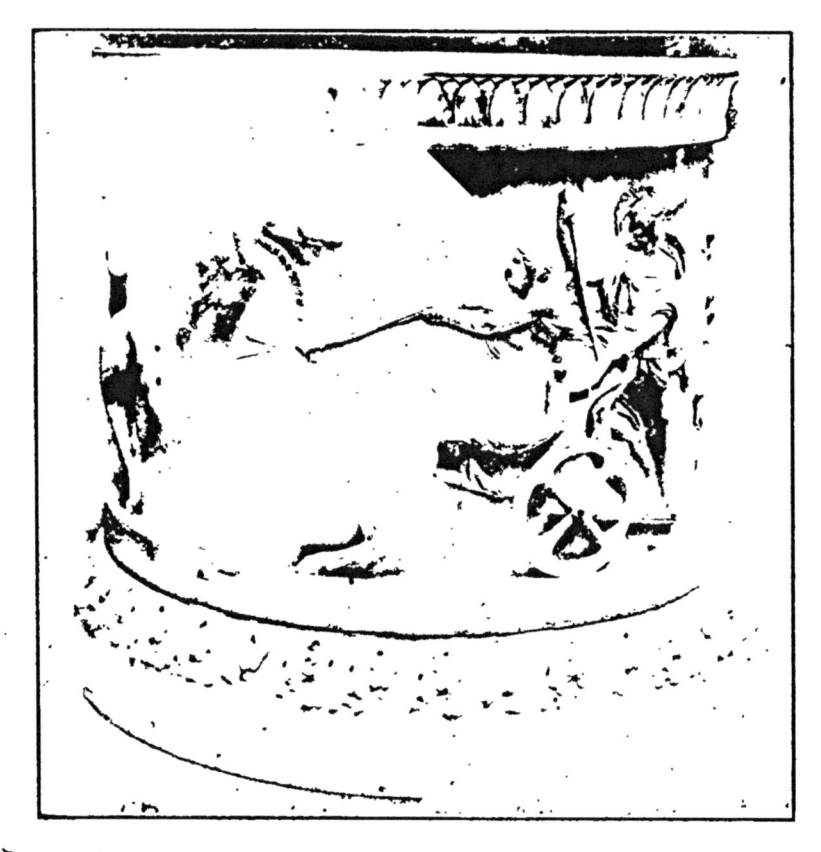

Fig. 54—Concrete Sun Dial Pedestal or Base for Table. Size 35 in. High by 38 in. in Diameter—Executed by the Erkins Studios

the inner pail should be kept about 2 inches from the bottom of the outer pail by letting it rest on a block of wood or a piece of brick. When

70 *Concrete Pottery and Garden Furniture*

Fig. 55—Glue Melting Pot on Stove showing Rack for Glue above

melting the glue do not have too hot a fire, but let the glue melt slowly until it is of the consistency of thin molasses. When it is of the proper consistency pour it into the funnel, which has previously been secured in place in the plaster

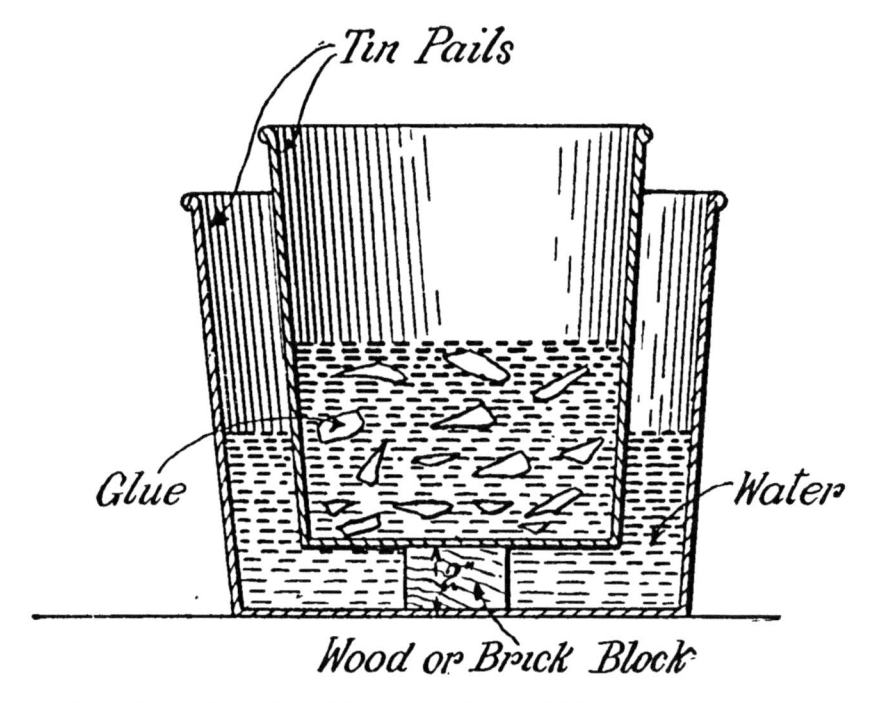

Fig. 56—Method of Making a Glue Melting Pot from two Tin Pails

case, as indicated in Fig. 51. Now as the mold fills up, the glue will run out of the vent holes, which are shown by the heavy dotted lines, thus indicating that the glue is flowing properly. As the glue appears at these holes, stop them up with a daub of modeler's clay. Keep on pouring the

72   Concrete Pottery and Garden Furniture

Fig. 57—Ornamental Figures—70 inches High—Executed by the Erkins Studios

Concrete Pottery and Garden Furniture 73

glue until it runs out of the highest vent hole and until the funnel remains full. The glue thus poured will take about twelve hours to congeal

Fig. 58 –Concrete Vase with Design in Relief—Executed by the Erkins Studios

or harden, after which time the plaster case or mask, as it is sometimes called, can be lifted off. This is done by first cutting the glue away from the funnel, and then removing the canvas straps which held the case down on the working board and prevented it from rising as the glue was poured. Now in turn remove the glue mold from the model. This can be easily done, if the model

Fig. 59—Highly Ornamented Concrete Table—By J. C. Kraus

has been properly oiled, by simply springing out the sides of the glue cast, and lifting it up from the face of the model.

Before making a cast in the glue mold, the face of it must be treated so as to make it as near waterproof as one can. A common method of doing this is to paint the surface of the mold with a saturated solution of alum. About three coats of this solution are necessary, letting each coat dry out well before applying the next. A simpler and probably more effective method is to coat the face of the glue mold with one or two coats of a fine grade of good clear flexible varnish. Before making a cast, always oil the inner face of the mold well with a light oil. To assemble the mold

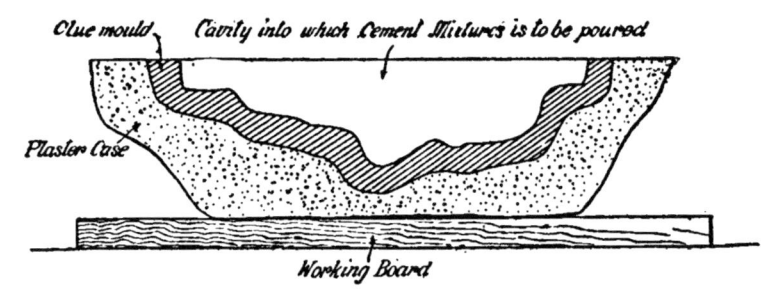

Fig. 60—Glue Mold Assembled and in Position for Pouring Cement

for a cast, place the mask or case on the working board, as shown in Fig. 60. Then drop in the glue mold, which will find its place in the case readily, and then proceed to pour in the cement mixture. The mixture to use for this class of work should be composed of 1 part Portland cement to 2 or 3 parts of sand. Enough water should be added to make it of a creamy consistency or thin enough to pour. Fill the mold with this mixture flush with the top, and then jar the mold up and down two or three times to force

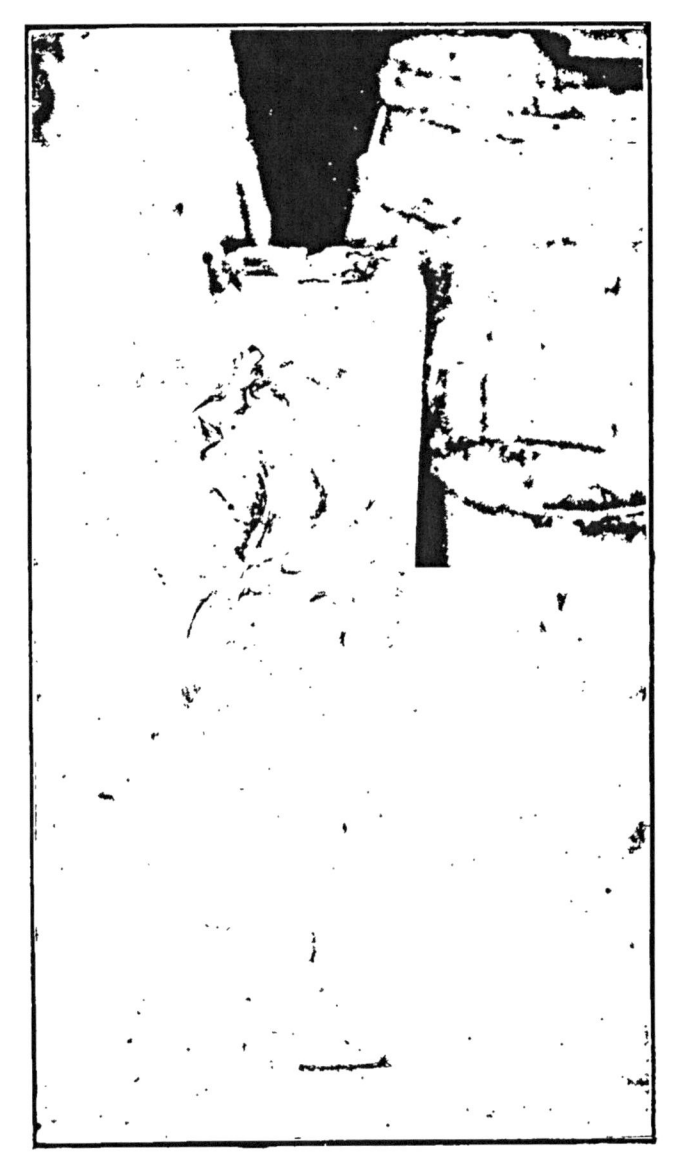

Fig. 61 - Plaster Model of Table Leg

out any air that may have gotten in with the mixture while pouring. If this is not done, air bubbles or voids may appear in the face of the finished cast. Allow this mixture to harden for at least twelve hours after being poured. To remove the cast, turn the case over, and the glue mold will come away from it; then by gently taking hold of the glue mold and bending it up, the cement cast will readily be released.

Fig. 62—First Operation in the Making of the Glue Mold

In making a glue mold for a piece having relief work on all four sides, or all around its surface, as in circular pieces, such as the table leg, the plaster model of which is shown in Fig. 61, a different method of procedure must be employed than that which has just been explained. The first thing to do is to place the model on the working board, as shown in Fig. 62. Now draw a line along the opposite sides of the model at its widest part, and build up to this line, from the

78 Concrete Pottery and Garden Furniture

working board, with modelers' clay. Sometimes in order to save clay and time, boards are placed along the sides of the model so as to come almost

Fig. 63--Half of Model Covered with Clay

Concrete Pottery and Garden Furniture 79

to a level with the line drawn on the model, and then the clay is built up from these boards to a line corresponding to the line on the model, as

Fig. 64—Plaster Case being Cast on Model over Clay

shown in Fig. 62. This line is known as the parting line.

After having built up the clay around the model as shown, a damp newspaper should be placed over it, and in turn this should be covered with a ½-inch layer of clay, as previously explained and as shown in Fig. 63. A plaster case should then be cast over this clay in a similar manner, as explained before and as shown in Fig. 64. After

Fig. 65—Model Turned Over and in Position to have Upper Half Covered with Clay

this case has hardened, the clay and boards, which were used for forming the parting line, should be removed and the whole piece, including the plaster case, the clay covering over the model, and the model itself, should be turned over on the working board into the position shown in Fig. 65. Now the upper part or half of the model, which is still exposed, is to be treated in like manner. Before casting the upper plaster cast, however, it would be well to shellac and oil the exposed edges of the lower plaster case, so as to prevent the upper half of the case sticking to it. After having cast the upper plaster case on the model, it will appear as shown in Fig. 66.

The whole should then be set up on end, and a

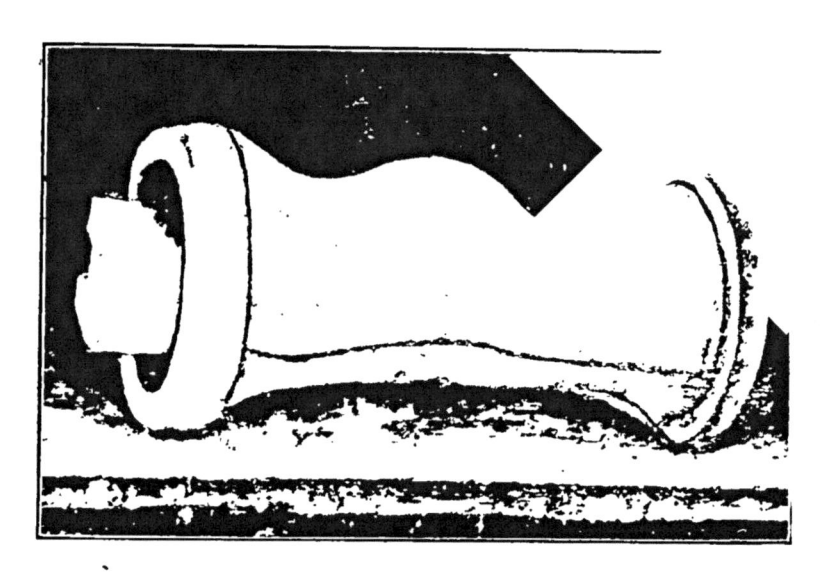

Fig. 66—Model Completely Covered with Clay and Plaster Case

plaster base or bottom should be cast on it. The inner sides of this bottom piece should be tapered and should extend up around the outer sides of the case for at least from 2 to 3 inches, as shown in Fig. 67. The method used for casting a plaster base or bottom of this kind for a mold is clearly explained in the chapter on "Plaster Molds." After having cast this bottom piece, the whole should be disassembled, and the plaster case,

82   *Concrete Pottery and Garden Furniture*

which was cast around the model, should be taken off, and the clay and paper in turn should be removed from the model. The model should

Fig. 67—Pouring the Glue into the Case and Around the Model

Concrete Pottery and Garden Furniture 83

then be thoroughly cleaned up and oiled. The plaster case should then be assembled around it, as shown in Fig. 67, and firmly held together by means of hooks or bands. The glue should then

Fig. 68—Showing the Flexibility of the Glue Mold

be poured into the cavity between the plaster case and the mold, as shown in the illustration. After having poured the glue, let the whole stand, without disturbing it in any way, for at least twelve hours, in which time the glue will have hardened sufficiently to allow of the two halves of the plaster case to be removed. These should come away readily from the glue if they have been well oiled before the glue was poured. On the outer part of the glue mold there will appear a line or a slightly elevated ridge of glue. This will indicate the location of the joining of the two halves of the plaster case. The glue mold must be cut along these lines, so as to form two halves of it. This cutting can be readily accomplished by using a good, strong, sharp knife. Do not hack it or roughen the edges of the glue any more than can be helped. The glue mold when cut in halves should appear as shown in Fig. 68. In the illustration one of the halves of the glue mold is shown in place in the plaster case, and the other is shown resting on the other half of the case. By the way it bends under its own weight, one can readily see how flexible it is. After having been cut in half, the inner surfaces of the glue mold should be treated with a saturated solution of alum, or it should be varnished, as previously explained. If the mold is to be varnished, it should be allowed to dry out for twenty-four hours after it has been removed from the model before the first coat is applied. It should then be well oiled before a cast is made in it. In assembling the mold for a cast, the two halves of the glue mold should be placed in their respective plaster cases. These in turn should then be

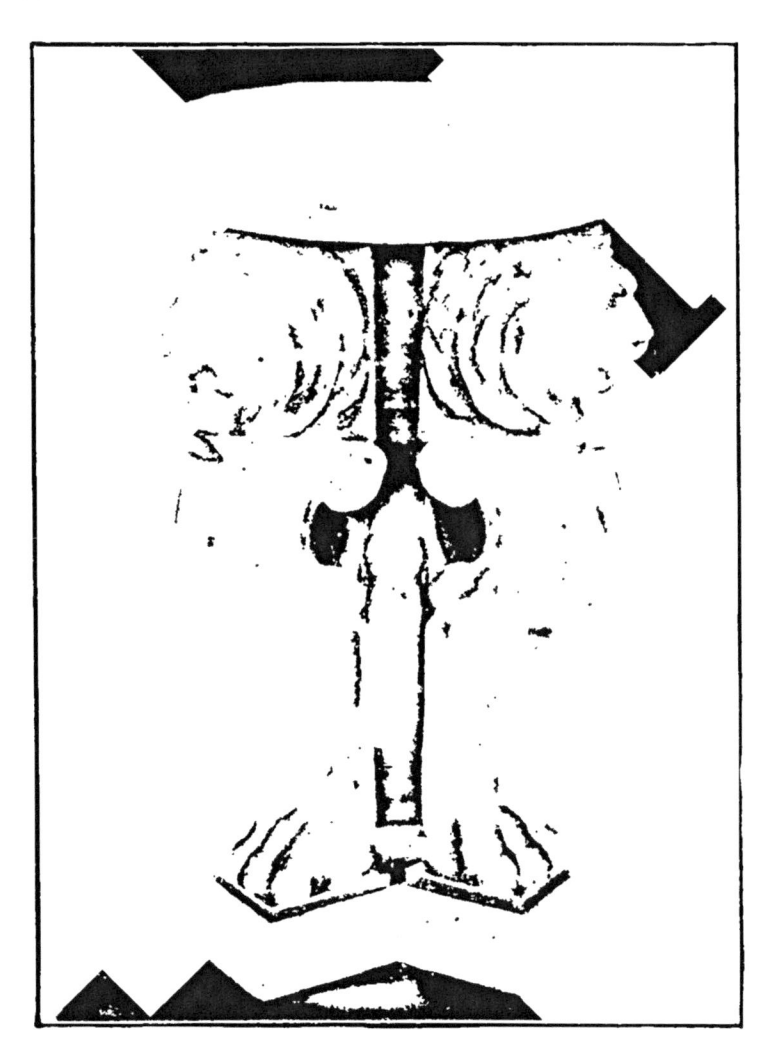

Fig. 69—Concrete Table, the Legs of which were Cast in a Glue Mold

brought together and placed in the bottom part of the mold, then they should be firmly secured together by means of bands or hooks, as was done when casting the glue mold and as illustrated in Fig. 67.

The pouring of the cement mixture, the removing of the mold, and the curing of the finished cast is done in a similar manner as when casting

Fig. 70—Large Vase and Saucer with Design in High Relief — Executed by J. C. Kraus

Concrete Pottery and Garden Furniture 87

in any other form of mold. In Fig. 69 is illustrated a table, the legs of which are of concrete casts made in the glue mold just described. The same principles of procedure as explained above are used in making glue molds for round or square vases. The only additional part required for vase work is the core. These can be made of

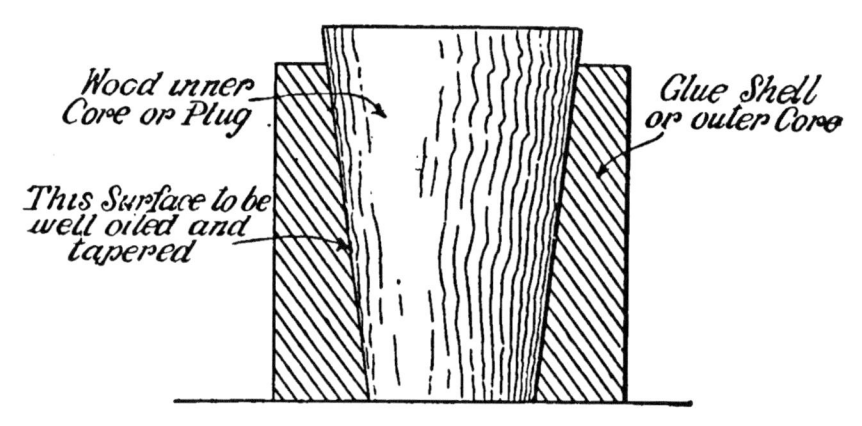

Fig 71 -Combination Glue and Wood Core for Vase Work

plaster as described in a previous chapter, or they can be made of glue with an inner core of wood, as illustrated in Fig. 71. In this case the outer part of the inner wood core should be well oiled, so that it can be withdrawn from the glue shell. The glue shell of the core, which will then remain in place in the cast, can then, due to its flexible nature, be collapsed and withdrawn from the inner part of the cast. When casting vases, always cast them with the bottom up, as explained in Chapters III and IV.

When one is through with a glue mold, it need

not be thrown away, for the glue in it is still good to use. It should be cut up into small pieces and allowed to dry out. It can then be melted over again and used for making other glue molds. A rack containing pieces of old glue molds cut up, ready for use, is shown in Fig. 55, just above the glue pots and stove.

CHAPTER VII.

COLORED CEMENTS AND METHODS USED IN PRODUCING DESIGNS WITH SAME

After having mastered the process of modeling and casting, as explained in the previous chapters, the craftsman can now take up the decorative features. The possibilities of ornamentation, one can say, are almost unlimited with this material. Various effects can be obtained. One can repro-

Fig. 72—Copy of an Antique—Executed by the Author

duce antiques which can hardly be told from the originals, and original designs embodying various colors can be made which will compare favorably with modern clay pottery effects. Owing to the material used the texture obtained is one which is full of life and sparkle. It has a distinct characteristic of its own which cannot be obtained in any other material.

As a specific case of what can be done along these lines we will take the copy of an antique which is illustrated in Fig. 72. This was made as follows: It was first cast with perfectly smooth sides, a mixture of 1 part Portland cement to 2 parts of fairly coarse brown sand being used. After pouring this mixture it was allowed to set in the mold for from eight to twelve hours. The mold was then removed and the piece was found to be in a more or less soft state. That is, it had to be handled carefully, and the concrete had not become so hard that an impression could not be made in it with the sharp point of a knife; the design as shown was then marked on the surface, and in turn it was cut and dug out by a strong knife blade. A straightedge was placed along the various lines, being used as a guide for the blade. The depth to which the design should be cut varies according to the size of the piece; but in small work usually from ⅛ of an inch to 3/16 of an inch will give the most effective results. If for any reason one cannot commence the work of cutting out the design within twelve hours after the piece has been cast, or until the piece has become quite hard, it will then be necessary to use a small hammer and chisel with which to cut out the design. Care should be taken, however, in using these tools not to strike too hard a blow, for if one hits too hard the piece may break, although in antique work if the edges of the cutout design are more or less irregular it makes the piece so much more effective.

In preparing any article for color inlay work,

Fig. 73—Vase with Elaborate Color Design—Executed by the Author

which has been modeled and built up on wire forms as explained in Chapters I. and II., such as a vase or other piece, as illustrated in Fig. 73, the design must be cut out previous to the inlaying of the colors exactly as has been just described for antique relief work.

If, however, the piece to be inlaid is to be made

in a mold as described in Chapters III. and IV., the mold can be prepared to form the desired depression, in which case the design will be cast in the piece. For complicated designs of this character a clay model must be provided from which the plaster mold is made. But in simple designs such as illustrated the piece which is to form the recess can be attached to the inside of the outside mold as shown in Fig. 75. This can be made of wood and can be secured in place by

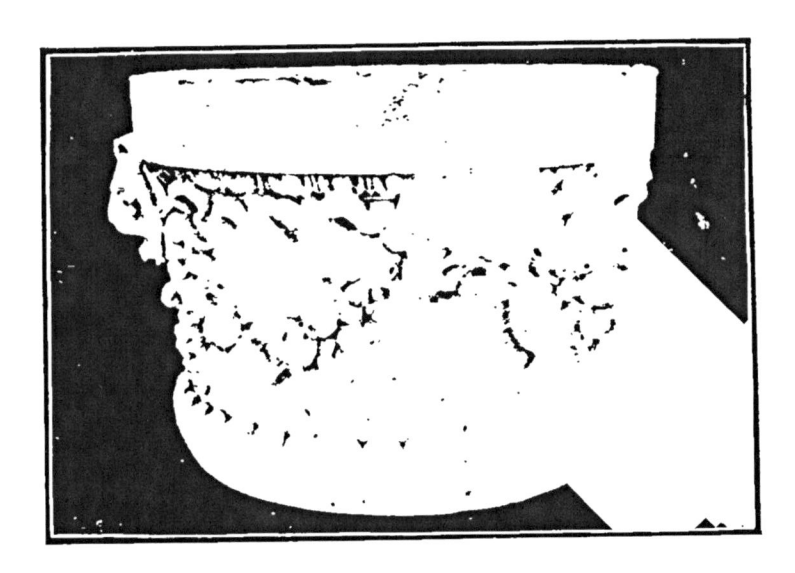

Fig. 74—Pompeian Vase—Executed by L'Ibal & Co.

brads. It should be located in the proper position and should be of the exact size and shape of the outline of the design and at least ⅛ of an inch thick. Shellac and oil the piece well before pouring the cement and allow a good bevel or draft on all of the edges so that it will draw out easily from the cast and thus leave a good, clean, sharp edge to the cavity into which to lay the colored cements.

A great many attempts have been made to produce satisfactory color work in cement, but until

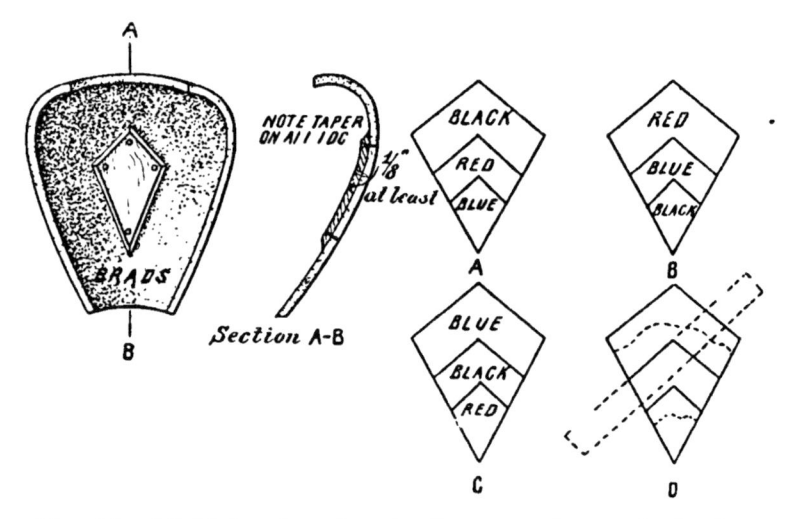

Fig. 75—Mold for Forming the Recess and Steps in Laying the Colored Cements

of late these attempts have been most unsatisfactory. This was largely due to the fact that ordinary Portland cement is of a gray color and on mixing it with the various color pigments the result was a decidedly dirty or dead tint of the color used, similar to that which would be produced in water colors by mixing them with water which had already been discolored by India ink or lampblack. Another cause of unsatisfactory results along these lines was the fact that many of those who experimented did not use the proper color pigments, the result being that the colors faded out on exposure to the weather. The first cause of not being able to produce true tints can now be overcome by the fact that a really true white Portland cement is being manufactured. This now can be procured from almost any cement dealer. By using this as a base with which to mix the pigments, true, clear colors can be obtained, and by the use of nothing but good mineral pigments, known as lime or cement-proof colors, it is possible to produce shades which will be absolutely permanent.

The writer has experimented largely with coloring matters from this country as well as from abroad. Many of the coloring matters obtained from abroad are very good, but their cost is naturally higher than those which are made in this country.

As before stated, mineral colors are those which give the best and most permanent results. They all come in powdered form and should be mixed with the dry cement and marble dust or white sand, as the case may be, until the whole mass is of a uniform tint throughout. After having mixed them as above, water should be added and the whole mixed into a mortar.

The following pigments, which can be procured from almost any of the large manufacturers or dealers in dry colors, will give satisfactory and permanent results:

Dry Pigments	Resulting Color
Red oxide of iron / Venetian red	Red
White Portland cement	White
Ultramarine blue / Oxide of cobalt	Blue
Chromate of lead / Yellow ocher	Yellow
Chrome oxide of copper	Green, light
Carbonate of copper	Green, dark
Lampblack / Torch black / Black oxide of copper	Black or Gray (according to quantity used.)
Ordinary Portland cement	Gray
Burnt umber	Brown

The amount of coloring matter to use in proportion to the cement depends entirely upon the depth or shade of the color desired. By mixing up small specimens of the color with various proportions of cement and making small test pieces of mortar and then noting the color of these after they have dried out, one can readily determine the proper amount of coloring matter to use. It is always better to weigh the amount of pigment used rather than to judge the amount by bulk, for by weighing a much more uniform result can be obtained.

For ornamental work where a wide range of colors is desired they can be procured by the same means as is used in water or oil color painting; that is, by mixing together the three primary colors, which are red, yellow, and blue. From these three colors can be obtained every color or tone that may be required. Thus blue mixed with yellow produces green; blue mixed with red produces violet, and red mixed with yellow produces orange, etc. In combining the coloring matters, always do so while they are in a dry state and thoroughly mix or grind them together before adding them to the white cement.

The method of laying these colored cement mortars in the design is as follows: First, enough water must be added to the dry mass to allow it to be mixed to the consistency of a thin paste. Then the design, which has already been cut out as previously explained, should be thoroughly wet down by sprinkling with a wet brush.

If a varicolored design is to be inlaid, it is always well to lay in all of one color at the same time, as is illustrated in Fig. 75. In this case we have figures *A, B* and *C* which are to contain the colors red, blue, and black, as indicated. First, with the aid of a blade of a penknife or any other handy tool according to the size of the work, lay the red cement in the design *A* as shown at *D* by the dotted lines. Let it come level with or even a trifle higher than the face or body of the vase or piece which is being inlaid; also let the colored cement project beyond its position in the finished design as indicated by the dotted lines. Now turn the vase around, and lay the red cement in the designs *B* and *C*, letting it project beyond its position as was done in the design *A*. The red cement which has been laid in the design *A* will now be set enough so that a straightedge made of a

Fig. 76—A Good Example of Colored Concrete Work—
Executed by the Author

flexible piece of wood, or other material such as cardboard, can be placed over it in the position of the finished design as indicated at *D* by the dotted lines.

The sharp edge of a knife can now be used to cut away the surplus cement which projects beyond the edge of the straightedge. In cutting away the surplus cement always cut away from the finished design. Proceed to cut away all other surplus cement from the other three sides of the design as just described and then in turn treat the designs *B* and *C* in the same manner. Now lay in the blue cement in all of the designs in a similar manner and then the black cement. If by chance any of the colored cements have gone beyond the designs and onto the face of the vase, scrape them

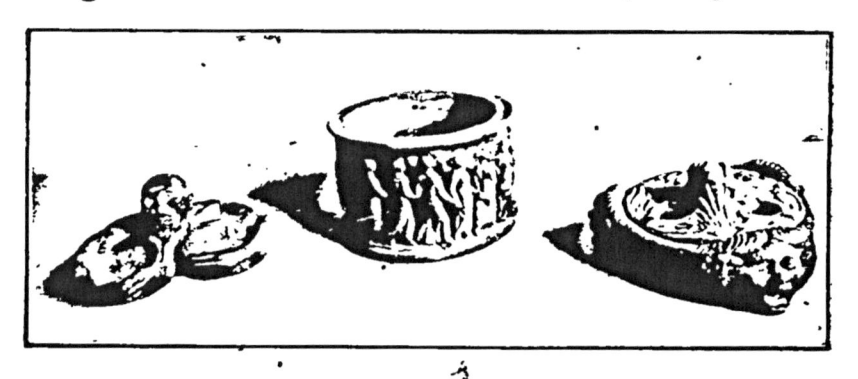

Fig. 77—Small Articles such as Fern-Jars, Pin-holders and Ash Receivers of Concrete make Attractive Ornaments—
Executed by J. C. Kraus

off before they harden and then with the back of the blade of the knife, which is more or less blunt, run around the outline of the designs as well as between the colors, using a straight edge as a guide. By doing this a distinct parting line is produced between each color and a better effect can be obtained.

The colored cements which have just been inlaid must, of course, be cured so as to harden them up. This is done by sprinkling them with water as explained in previous chapters.

CHAPTER VIII.

THE SELECTION OF AGGREGATES AND THE PREPARATION OF THE MIXTURE

In the previous chapters nothing much has been said in detail in regard to the numerous and various materials which can be used with which to make concrete, such as the different kinds of stones, pebbles, etc. Nor has anything been said in regard to the quantity of each ingredient necessary to make a fixed amount of finished material.

Concrete is made by mixing together with water various proportions of Portland cement, sand, and stone. The sand and stone which go to make part of the mixture are commonly known as aggregates. It is by the careful selection of these aggregates that we are able to produce numerous pleasing and artistic results.

In many cases, if the proper aggregates are used in the right proportion, natural stones such as limestone, granite of all colors, brownstone, and French Caen stone, etc., can be so closely simulated that it takes an expert to tell it from the real material.

The ordinary concrete or cement surface as usually seen is most uninteresting in appearance. As a general thing, it is smooth and lifeless and of a dull gray color. The same general appearance as just described for ordinary concrete will prevail in almost any concrete surface, no matter what the aggregate used, unless the surface is treated so as to expose or bring out the aggregates used. If, however, the surfaces of the concrete in which selected aggregates have been used are properly treated, a marked difference between these surfaces and those obtained with

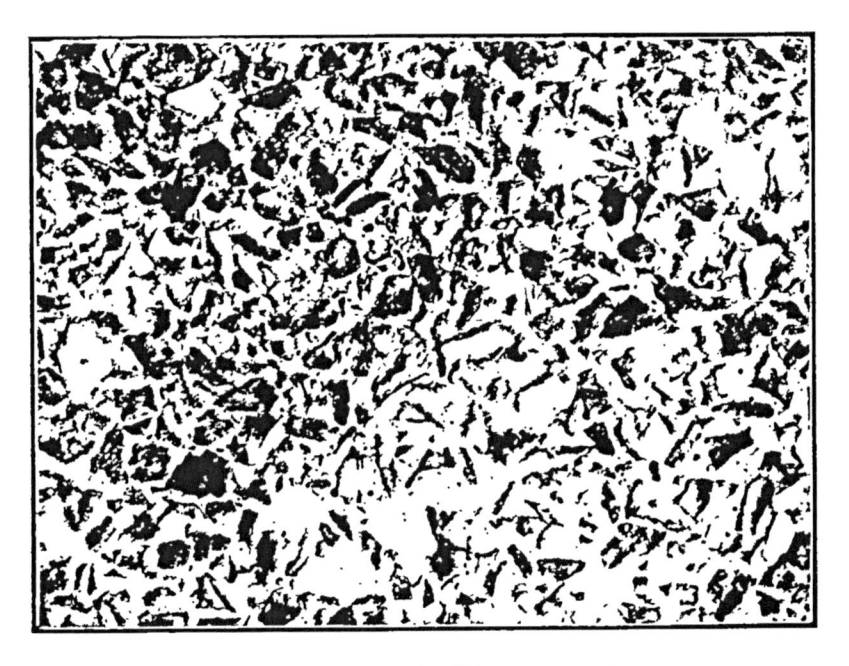

Fig. 78—Showing Texture obtained by using Selected Aggregates

ordinary mixtures will be noted. By varying the kind, size, and proportions of the aggregate used, surface finishes of practically any desired color and texture can be obtained, the possibilities being limited only by the number of different kinds of aggregates available and the combinations of the same.

In small work, that is, where the thickness of the finished product is to be ½ inch or less, never use any aggregate exceeding ⅛ inch in size, especially so if the mixture is to be made thin enough to pour. In larger work having a thickness of 1 inch or more, aggregates up to ¼ of an inch can be used with good results.

Some interesting textures for pottery work can be obtained from the following mixtures:

A mixture composed of 1 part white marble chips, not exceeding ¼ inch in size, and 1 part of trap rock or other dark stone of the same size mixed with 1 part of Portland cement and 1 part of marble dust will produce a surface similar in appearance to a light granite. This mixture should be allowed to set for twelve hours after pouring, then the molds should be carefully removed, as the concrete is still green, and the surface of the concrete should be lightly brushed with a stiff brush.

As the concrete is not thoroughly set or hardened yet, this operation will remove the surface cement, and thus expose the aggregates of marble and trap rock. After having performed the above operation, allow the piece to harden a few days, and then treat the surface with a solution composed of 1 part of commercial muriatic or hydrochloric acid to 3 parts of water. Dash this solution onto the face of the concrete surface with a brush, and allow it to remain for at least fifteen minutes. Then thoroughly scrub it off with a

good stiff brush and plenty of clean water. This
operation will remove all of the surplus cement,
and will leave a good clean surface full of life
and sparkle. Instead of using white marble-chips

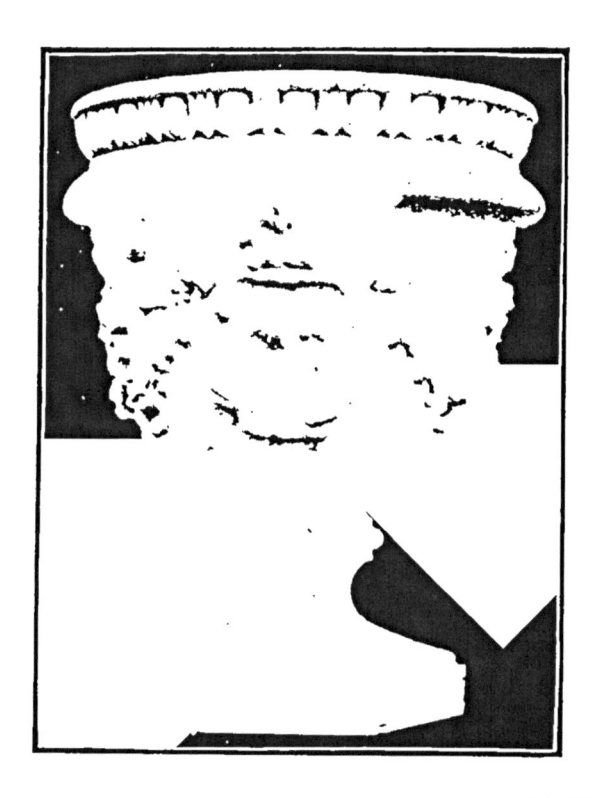

Fig. 79—Concrete Urn made with White Marble Dust
and Portland Cement—Executed by L'Ibal & Co.

and granite, as above, one can vary the results by
using white marble chips and crushed-up red
brick; or various colored marbles crushed to the
proper size can be used, and then by treating the
surfaces as explained, the colors in the various

aggregates will be exposed, thus producing some very interesting surfaces.

A good light-colored surface somewhat simulating limestone can be procured by using 1 part Portland cement to 2 or 3 parts of white marble dust. After this has become thoroughly hard, treat it with acid as described above. The acid will eat off any surface cement, and thus the marble dust will be exposed, producing a pleasing sparkle throughout the entire surface. To simulate white marble, use 1 part white Portland cement to 2 parts of marble dust, and treat surface with acid as described.

By incorporating in the above mixture a small amount of yellow ocher a pleasing buff tint will be given to the mass, which will then very closely resemble French Caen stone. To simulate red granite, use red granite chips or screenings. These can be procured at almost any stone yard where they cut granite. The pieces to use should range in size from ¼ inch down to dust. If the pieces available are too large, they can be crushed up with a hammer. The proportions of the mixture should be 1 part of Portland cement to 2 parts of the granite. After having set for twelve hours, brush the surface out and treat it with acid as already explained, and the surface thus obtained will very closely resemble the real red granite. From the above details the reader will have grasped the possibilities to be obtained by the selection of aggregates, and now by using a

104 *Concrete Pottery and Garden Furniture*

little ingenuity can without further instruction experiment along original lines, which will be found most fascinating work.

In regard to the amount of the various ingredients to use for a fixed amount of finished material, the uninitiated often think, and naturally so, that

Fig. 80—Large Flower Box, finished with Antique Stone Effect—Size of Box 24 in. high by 25 in. wide by 41 in. long, Legs 15 in. high—Executed by Erkins Studios

if an amount of finished material equal in bulk to three glassfuls is required, all that is necessary to do, if it be a 1 to 2 mixture, is to take one glassful of cement and two glassfuls of sand, and then by mixing these together they will still have an amount of material that will fill three glasses. This is not so. The particles of cement are ground so fine that the cement is practically one dense mass; but the particles of sand are coarser, and between each of the particles appears a space or cavity. These cavities are called voids, and it is in these voids that the larger portion of the cement finds its place when the mass is mixed. As the majority of sands used in concrete work contain from 25 per cent to 40 per cent of voids (we will take the larger figure for an example), it is plain then that each glass of sand contains about 40 per cent of voids. Therefore in two glassfuls of sand we will have 80 per cent of one glassful of voids. As we only have one glassful of cement to add to the two glassfuls of sand, and as the cement fills the 80 per cent of voids in the sand, it is plain that we have but 20 per cent left upon which we can figure for bulk. Therefore, instead of having three glassfuls of material, as one might naturally think, we will only have two glassfuls and 20 per cent of one glassful over, or two and one-fifth glassfuls of finished material. The percentage of voids varies largely in different grades of sands. The finer the particles of which the sand is made up, the smaller the percentage of voids. It is always best to use sand in which the particles are not uniform in size, or in other words, use what is commonly termed a well-graded sand. By this is meant a sand in which the

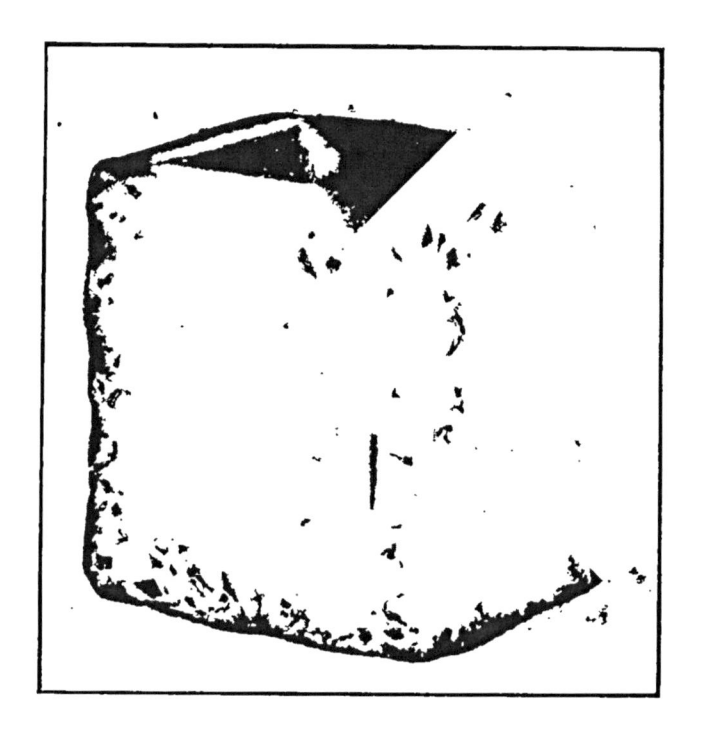

Fig. 81—Concrete Flower Box made with Selected Aggregates and Inlaid with Tile—Executed by Albert Moyer

particles vary in size say from 1/32 inch or smaller up to 1/16 inch or a trifle larger. The heavier the work, the coarser the sand that can be used. Be sure that the sand used is clean. By clean sand is meant sand that is free from loam or clay. One can readily detect dirty sand by placing same in the palm of the hand and slightly wetting it. Then if by rubbing it around the hand becomes discolored, there is more or less dirt in the sand. A little dirt will not do much harm, but it is always well to have it per-

Fig. 81a—Concrete Flower Box made with Selected Aggregates and Inlaid with Tile—Executed by Albert Moyer

fectly clean. It is often found necessary to wash the dirt out of sand by means of water. This can be done by placing the sand in a pail of water and agitating it, thus making the dirt rise to the top. To thoroughly wash the sand, keep running the water into the pail and agitating the sand until the water discharged is practically clear.

When using a stone aggregate in the mixture, the spaces or voids between the particles of stone are filled by the cement and sand in the mixture, as were the voids in the sand filled by the cement. As in sand, the larger the particles of stone used, the greater the percentage of voids in it will be. Therefore a greater amount of sand and cement will be required to fill them.

By a little experimenting along these lines, one will become experienced enough to judge fairly closely the amount of each ingredient to use in mixing up any amount of finished material needed. It is always well to mix a trifle more material than is needed rather than not enough. For when one once starts pouring a cast, they should continue to pour until the mold is full. If not, a mark is very apt to show in the finished cast where pouring was left off and started again. Never try to use any material that has been mixed and let stand for more than half an hour. For in this time the concrete will have commenced to get what is called its initial set. If the mass is now disturbed and worked up again, the product produced will never have the same strength as one made with freshly-mixed material. In mixing, always mix the cement and sand together thoroughly before adding the water. One can judge by the color of the mass, fairly well, as to whether the mixing is complete. If the color is uniform throughout, it is a pretty good sign that the aggregates are well distributed through the mass. When making a mixture containing cement, sand, and stone, always mix the cement and sand dry first and then add the stone, which has previously been well soaked in water. In this way one is assured of having each stone coated with the cement and sand; for as soon as the damp stone comes in contact with the dry cement and sand, it adheres to them and covers the stones completely; thus a compact matrix of cement and sand is formed between each and every particle of stone, and binds them securely together into a dense and compact mass.

CHAPTER IX.

WOODEN MOLDS

The accompanying illustrations show some interesting examples of decorative flower pots. These look as though they were difficult to produce, but they are easy to make when one knows how. The first thing to do is to prepare a mold. Figs. 83, 84, and 85 show detail drawings of a wooden mold for a flower pot 9 inches square by 10 inches high, and Figs. 86 and 87 show half-tone illustrations of a wooden mold for a pot 14 inches

Fig. 82—Good Examples of Hand Modeled Vases, Inlaid with Hand Made Moravian Tile—Executed by Frank Nahodyl

square by 18 inches high. It will be noticed that the cores in both of these cases are different. The collapsible core, shown in Fig. 84, is undoubtedly the best, as there is less fear of breaking the cast when removing it. It takes a trifle longer to make, but in the end it will pay. After complet-

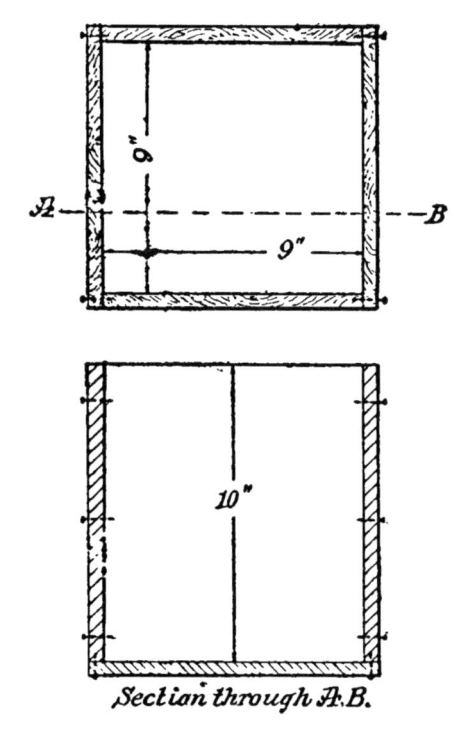

Fig. 83—The Outside Form of the Flower Pot Mold

ing the mold, the concrete mixture should be made up. It should consist of 1 part Portland cement and from 2 to 3 parts of sand or marble dust. These should be mixed together dry as previously explained, and enough water added to make it of

112 *Concrete Pottery and Garden Furniture*

the consistency of a thin putty or heavy cream. The next operation after mixing is the placing of this plastic mass into the mold. This is done as follows: First fill the mold solid up to a level with the bottom of the core, pack the cement down well, and then place the core box in position,

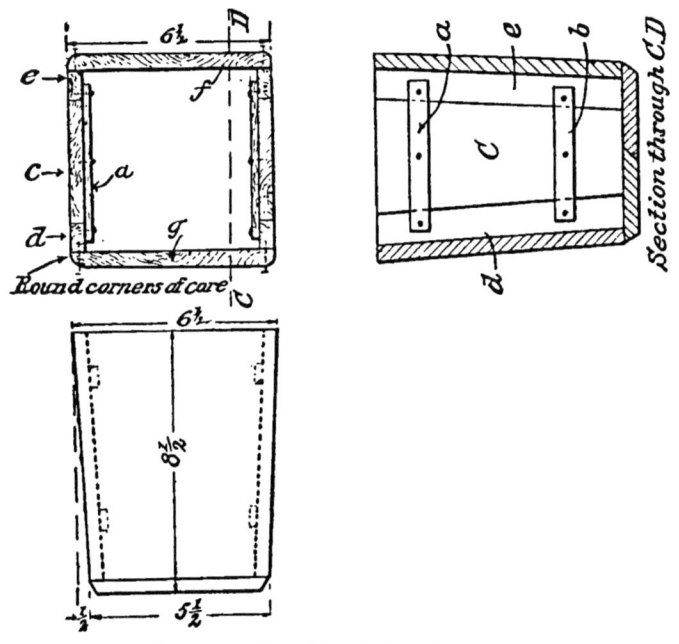

Fig. 84—Details of the Core Box

as shown is Figs. 85 and 86. Be sure that it is centered in the box. This is important, for if the core is not exactly in the center, the sides of the pot will not be of equal thickness.

A good way to center and secure the core in position is to nail a strip of wood to it, and in turn nail the ends of this strip to the top of the outside form, as shown in Figs. 85 and 86. After the mold has been placed and secured as above, fill the rest of the mold with the plastic concrete. When the mixture reaches the top of the mold

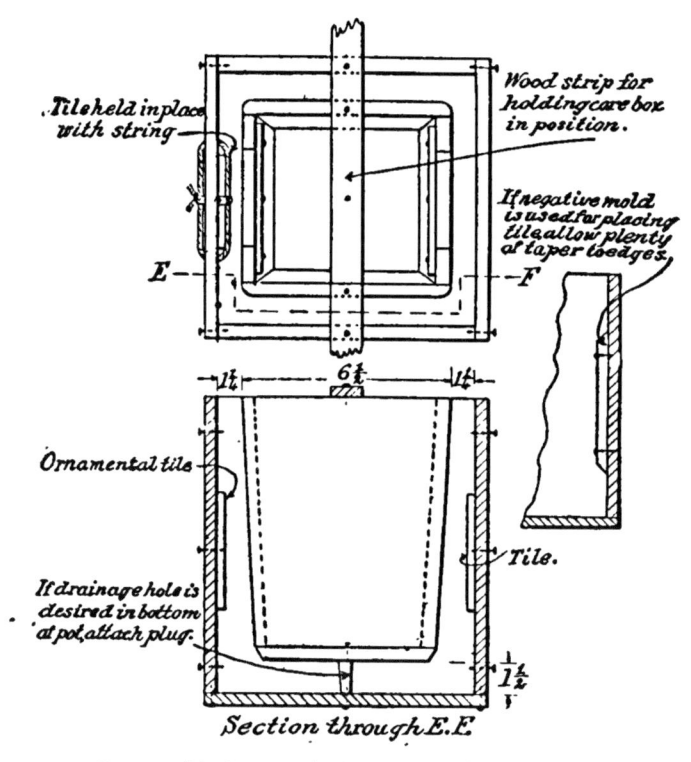

Fig. 85—The Mold Assembled for the Placing of the Concrete

smooth it off nicely, and set the mold and its contents on a level place to let the concrete set or harden. In about twelve hours from the time of pouring (do not let it be longer than this, for if so the concrete will be too hard for treatment) the concrete will be sufficiently hard to remove the molds. This should be done carefully, in order not to break the corners, as the concrete is yet more or less soft. In removing the mold, take

Fig. 86—Mold Assembled—Front Side of Outer Mold off to Show Core Box

the core out first. To do this, first remove the small strips *a* and *b*, which have been nailed from the inside, as indicated in Fig. 84. On removing these strips, the V-shaped sections *c* will be released from the sections *d* and *e*, and can then be forced toward the center of the pot and drawn out. After these V-shaped sections have been

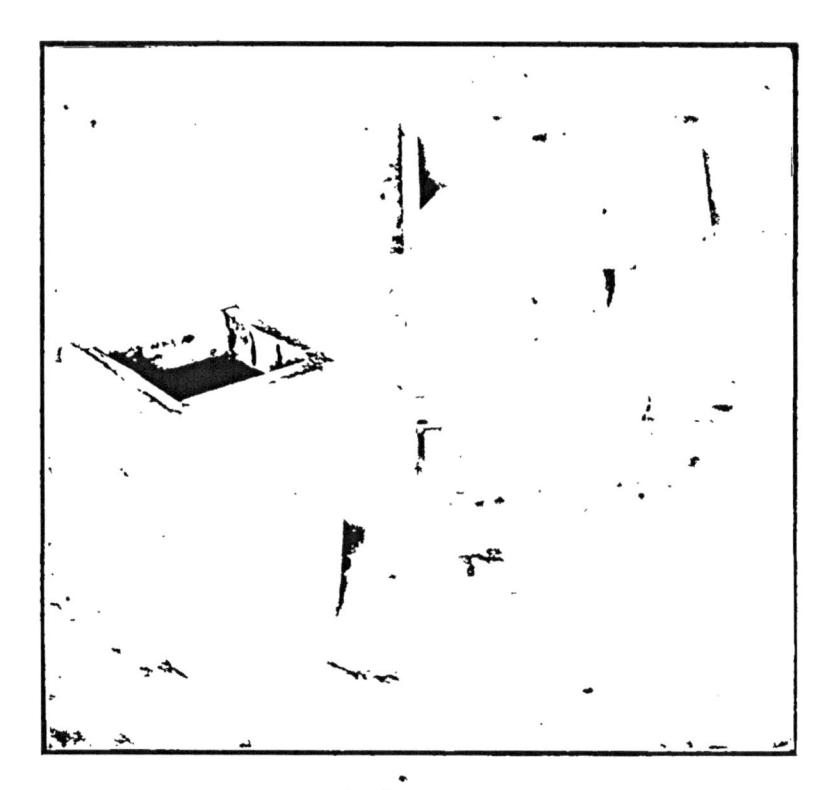

Fig. 87—Showing Separate Pieces of Mold

removed, the sides *f* will be free, and can be collapsed toward the center of the box and in turn can be removed. The bottom, which is made in two pieces, as shown, will then release itself freely. It would be well to grease the outer part of the core before placing the concrete, as this will allow of the core being released more readily than if it were not done. If a solid core is used, as indicated in Fig. 86, a direct pull must be given to remove it from the cast. The best way to remove a core of this kind is shown in Fig. 88. In Fig. 89 is shown an illustration of the cast after it has been removed from the mold. The outline of a design has been drawn on it, and the modeler

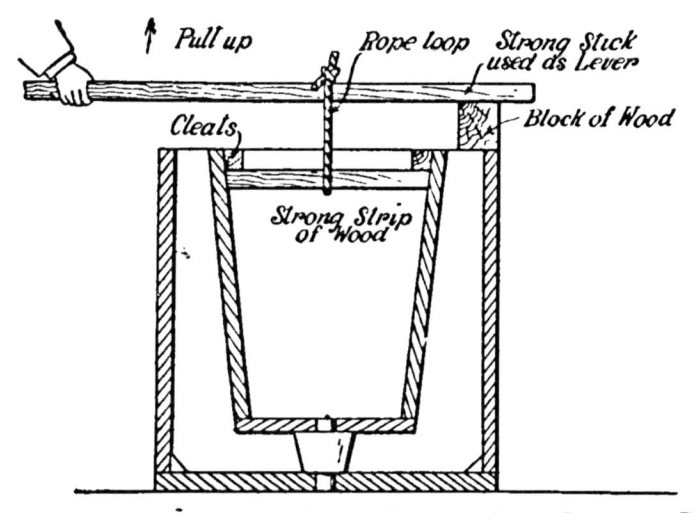

Fig. 88—Method of Removing Solid Core from Concrete Cast

is just starting to cut the design out. As the concrete is still in a soft state, this can be readily done by scraping the surface with steel tools of the proper shape. Fig. 90 shows the piece after the modeling is practically finished. The modeler is shown here in the act of touching up some of the finer detail. Fig. 82 shows two pots cast in the same mold as described above. These pots

Concrete Pottery and Garden Furniture 117

are also modeled by hand, after being taken from the mold, but in addition to the modeling they are also embellished with hand-made Moravian tile. There are various methods employed for inserting these tiles in the outer surfaces of the pots.

Fig. 89—Cast of Box after being Removed from Mold

A simple method for doing this is to place in the inner surface of the outer mold a negative mold. This negative mold is made of wood and should be of the exact shape, but a trifle larger in size than that of the tile which is to be inserted.

Fig. 90—Cast of Box after Modeling is Complete

Concrete Pottery and Garden Furniture 119

These negative molds can be nailed in the desired position to the inside of the outer mold, and then on drawing or stripping the outer mold from the cast, a cavity will be left in the outer surface of the pot, into which the tiles can be cemented in place.

Another method of placing the tiles in place is

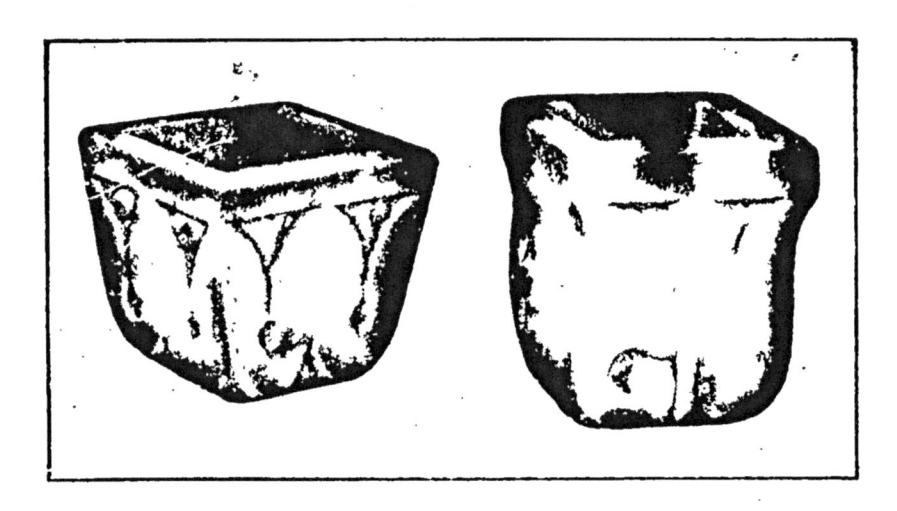

Fig. 91—Hand Modeled Vases—Executed in Dark Green Cement by Frank Nahodyl

to bore small holes through the outer forms, and secure the tiles in their proper position on the inside of the outer forms by tying them in place by string as indicated in Fig. 85, care being taken to see that the ornate side of the tile is placed next to the wood. The concrete is then poured the same as though an unornamented pot was being cast. Before removing the outer forms in this case, however, the strings which hold the tile in place should be cut. This is perhaps an easier method of placing the tile than that of making a negative mold. But in some cases it is hard to

Fig. 92—Vase made with White Marble Chips and Trap Rock inlaid with Moravian Tile—Executed by Albert Moyer

get the plastic concrete to flow completely around the tile. If in removing the forms, however, it is found that there are some places where the concrete has not run up to the tile, these holes or voids as they are called can be filled in or pointed up with cement mortar. This method of making pots or vases will be found most interesting, as it is suggestive of an unlimited number of designs and combinations. each of which will contain more or less individuality,

CHAPTER X.

GARDEN FURNITURE—CONCRETE PEDESTALS

Sun dials, statuettes, and vases mounted on ornamental pedestals add greatly to the picturesqueness of the modern garden. These pedes-

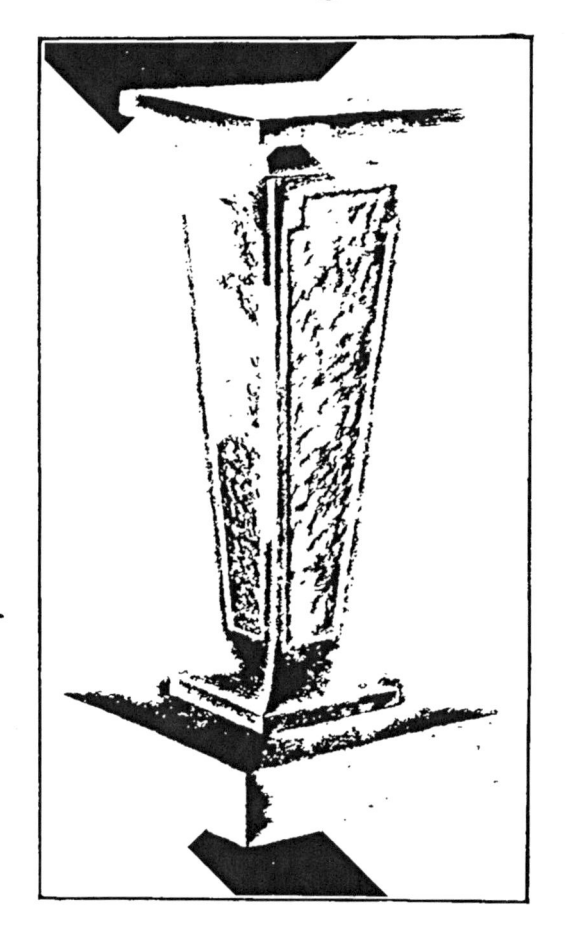

Fig. 93 – Concrete Pedestal—Executed by the Author

tals are made in numerous designs and of various materials, such as stone, marble, and concrete.

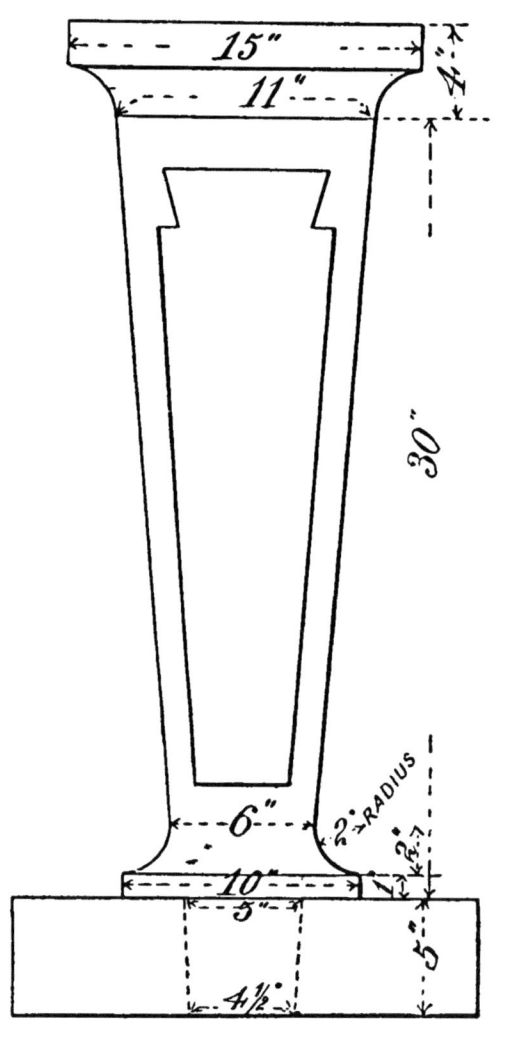

Fig. 94—Outline Sketch, Showing Dimensions

The accompanying half-tone illustration, Fig. 93, shows a pedestal made of white Portland cement.

It is of simple design, and one which lends itself nicely to the material, inasmuch as the forms in

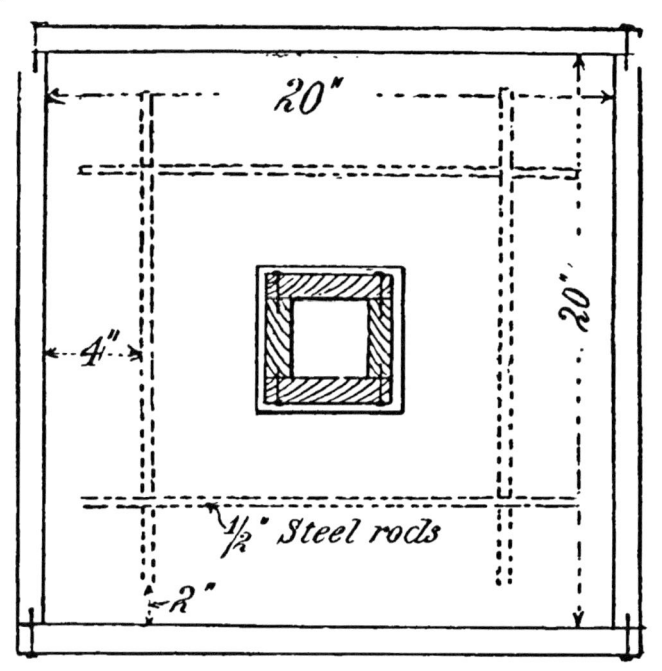

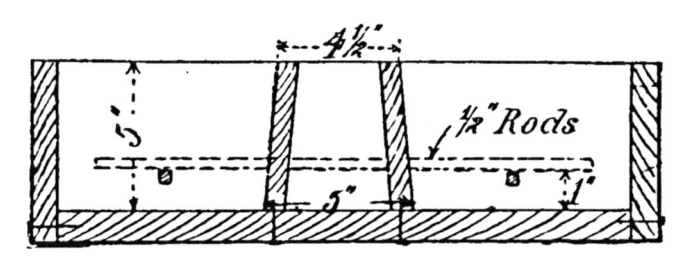

Fig. 95—Detail of Base Mold

which to cast it are easily made. Fig. 94 is an outline sketch of the pedestal, in which are given its general dimensions, and Figs. 95, 97, 98, 100,

Concrete Pottery and Garden Furniture 125

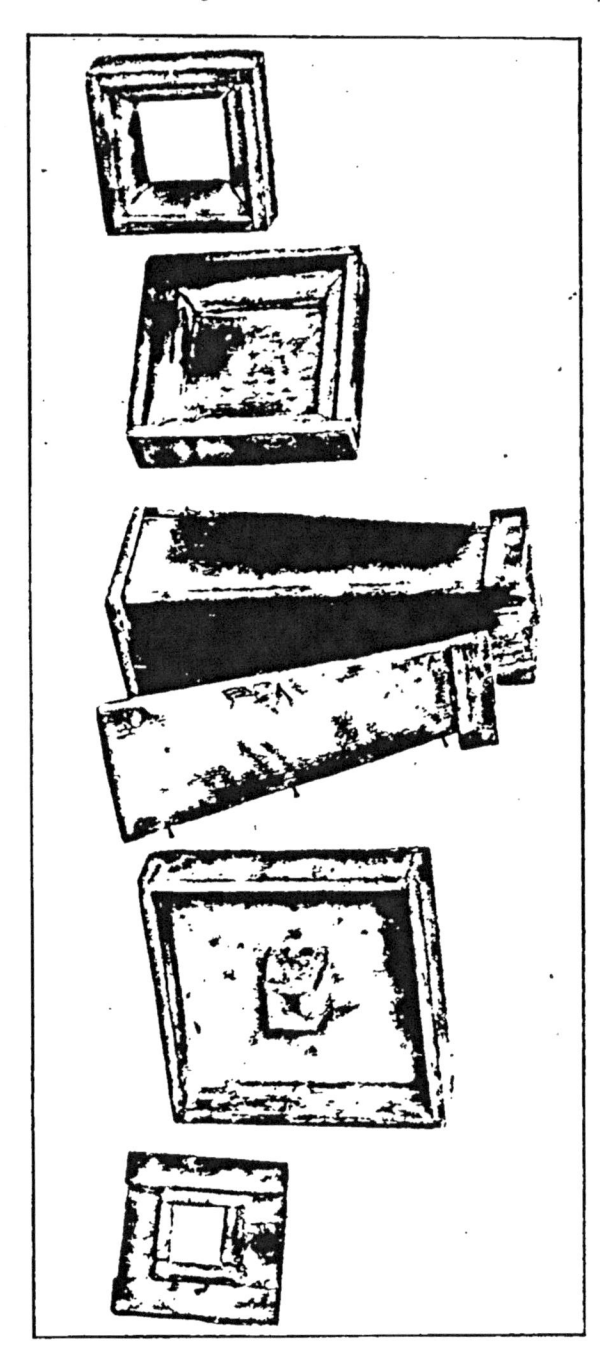

Fig. 96—Parts of Mold Before Assembling

and 102 show details of the molds in which it is cast. Fig. 96 shows the various parts of the mold before assembling. Fig. 99 shows the shaft mold

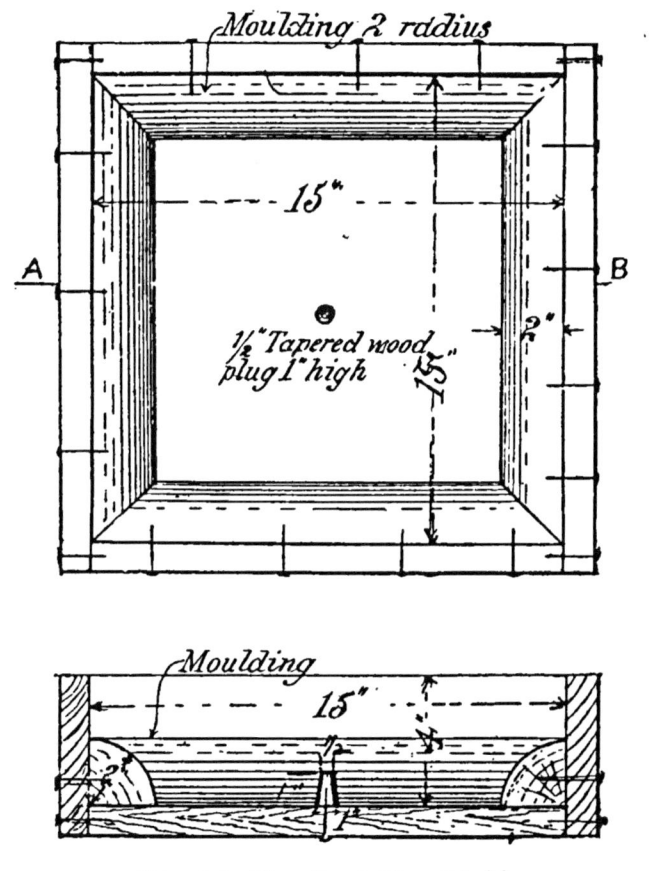

Fig. 97—Detail of Cap Mold

assembled in position ready to pour, and Fig. 101 shows the three finished pieces of the pedestal before setting them up.

The molds should all be made of 1-inch lumber, and the dimensions given should be followed closely. The base mold shown in Fig. 95 consists of nothing more or less than a square box with

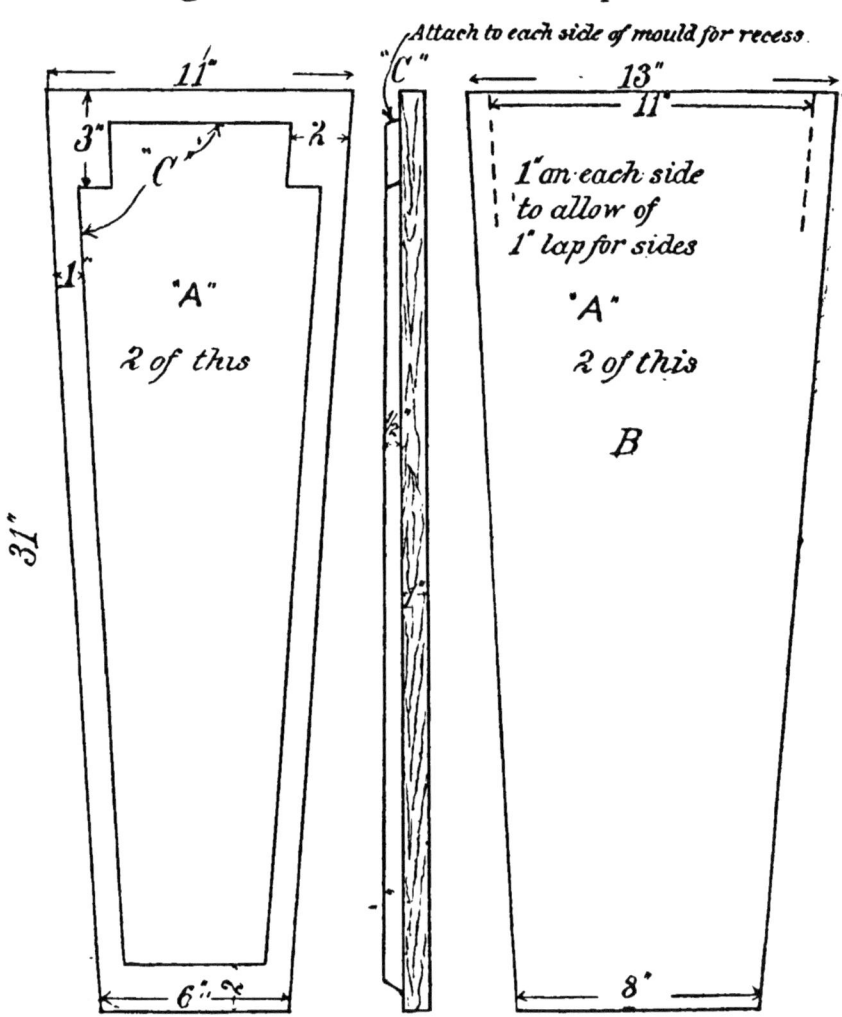

Fig. 98—Detail of Main Part of Shaft Mold

sides 5 inches high. In the center of the bottom of this box is placed a tapered core, so as to produce a hole in the cast to correspond in size to the outside dimensions of the plug on the bottom of the shaft of the pedestal, as shown in Fig. 101. The mold for the top or cap of the pedestal is

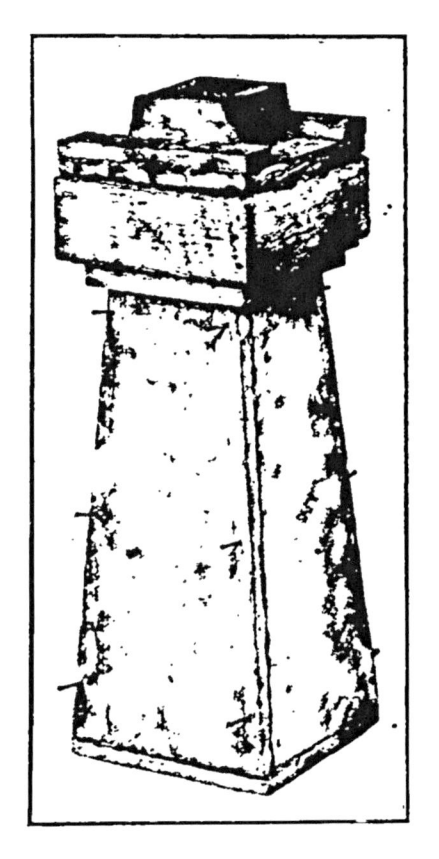

Fig. 99—Shaft Mold Assembled and in Position Ready to Pour

shown in Fig. 97. This like the base mold is merely a square box. It is 4 inches deep, and a ½-inch tapered plug is placed in the center of its bottom as shown, in order to produce a ½-inch hole in the bottom of the cap in which to insert the ½-inch reinforcing rod, which passes through the entire length of the shaft, as shown in the assembled drawing, Fig. 102. Strips of 2-inch quarter-round stock molding mitered at the corners, as shown, are placed in the bottom of this

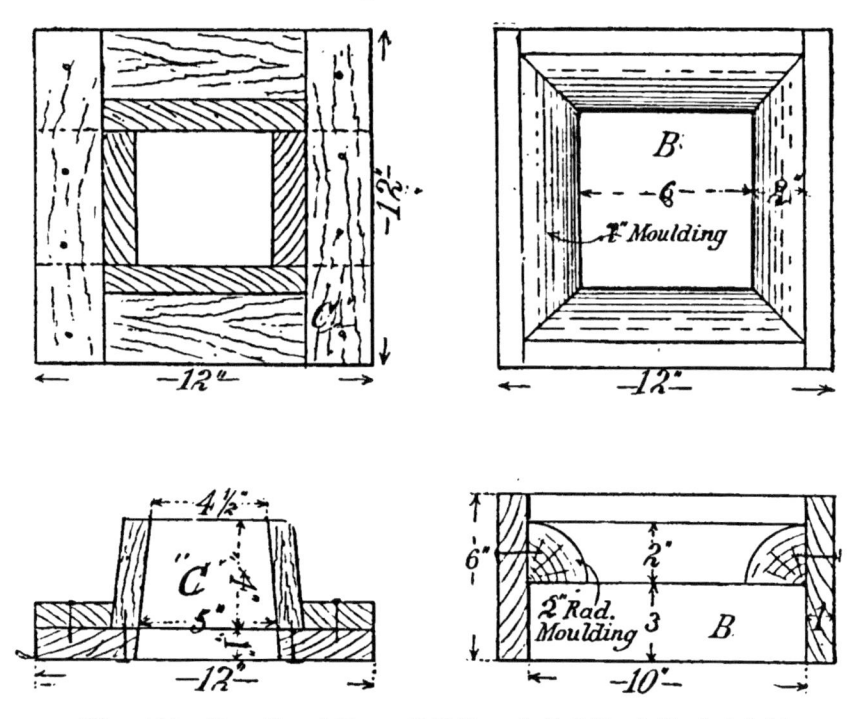

Fig. 100—Details of Parts "B" and "C" of Shaft Mold

mold in order to give the desired outline to the lower portion of the cap. The main shaft mold is made in three pieces, as shown in Fig. 102. Fig. 98 shows the details of the sides of the main part of the shaft mold. The recessed panels shown in the sides of the pedestal in Fig. 93 can either be

130   Concrete Pottery and Garden Furniture

Fig. 101—Pieces of Pedestal Before Assembling

cast in or it can be tooled out, after the pedestal has been cast, by means of chipping with a ham-

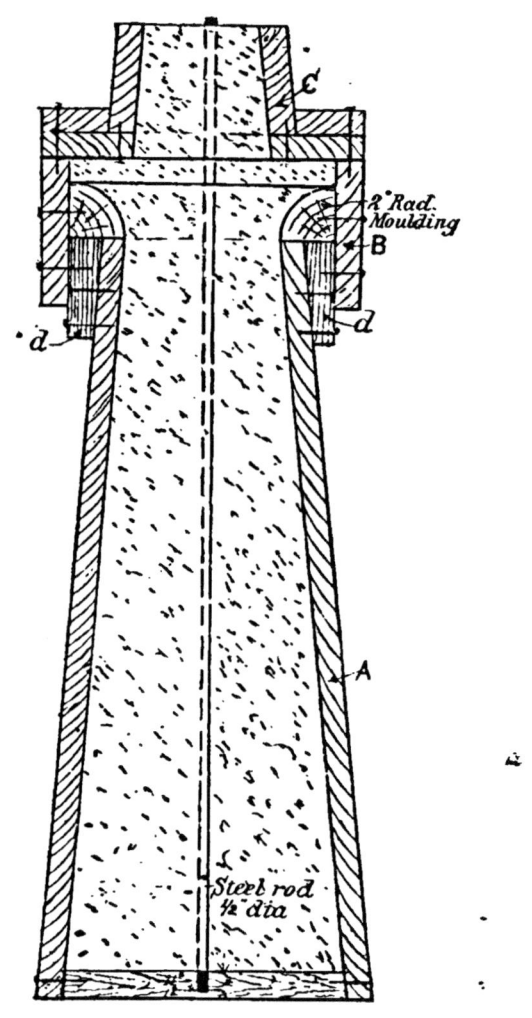

Fig. 102—Showing Assembled Mold in which to Cast Shaft

mer and chisel. If it is desired to cast it in, rather than to tool it out, a panel or negative mold, as shown at *C*, Fig. 98, should be attached to the inner side of each side of the shaft mold as shown. The edges of this negative mold for the panel should be beveled off as indicated in the sectional drawing, so as to allow it to be released readily from the cast when removing the forms. Details of parts *B* and *C* of the shaft mold are shown in Fig. 100. Part *B* is a bottomless box 10 inches square on the inside, with sides 6 inches high, and in it are secured, on all four sides, and mitered at the corners as shown, pieces of 2-inch quarter-round stock molding. These are securely fastened to the sides 1 inch from the top. Part *C* of the mold is made of four pieces of 1-inch board as shown, on which is built up the cone which forms the lug on the bottom of the shaft. Part *A* of the mold at its top should have secured to it, on all four sides, pieces of 2-inch by 1-inch tapered strips, as shown by the shaded portion at *d* in Fig. 102. The outside dimensions of these strips should be such that the inner portion of part *B* fits over them snugly.

The bottom of part *A* of the mold should have a 9/16-inch hole ½ inch deep bored in its center in which to place the ½-inch steel reinforcing rod, as shown. After having completed the various parts of the mold as described above, sandpaper the inner surfaces of them and give them two coats of shellac; let this dry thoroughly, and then oil the inside surface well with a fairly thin oil. Now assemble the shaft mold, letting section *A* stand

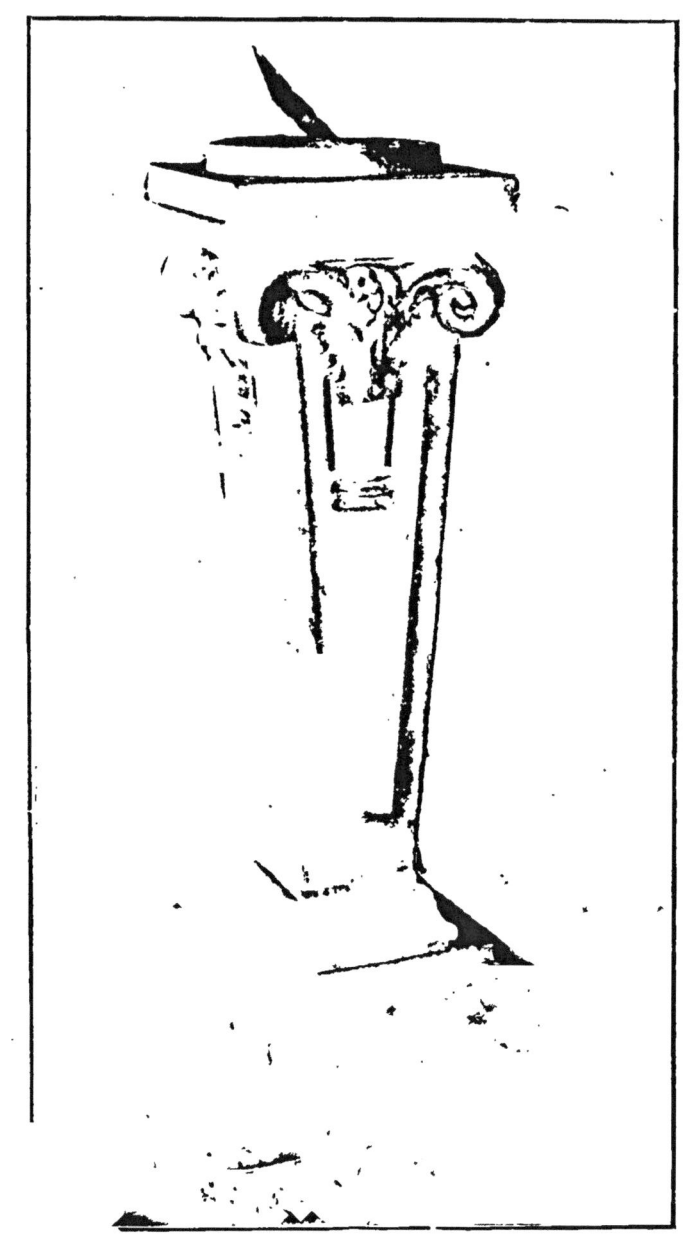

Fig. 103—Showing Pedestal with Relief Design—Executed by the Rowley Studios

on end, as shown in Fig. 102. Place section *B* in position as shown, care being taken to let the quarter-round molding rest snugly down on the pieces *d* of section *A*. Then place the steel rod in position, and commence to deposit the concrete mixture. If a white shaft is desired, use one part of white Portland cement and two parts of white marble screenings ranging in size from dust up to ⅜ inch. Mix these together dry, and then add enough water to make a fairly thick paste. Fill the mold flush with the top of part *B*, tapping the sides and jarring part *A* of the mold occasionally to settle the concrete mixture as it is being deposited. When the concrete is flush with the top of section *B*, place section *C* in position, and proceed to fill it flush with the top. Allow the concrete to set or harden in the molds for at least twenty-four hours before attempting to remove the molds. In securing the molds together use as few nails as possible, and in removing the mold from the cast, great care must be taken in loosening them, so as not to injure the casts. In removing the shaft mold, take off part *C* first, then part *B*, and finally section *A*. The base and cap molds should be filled with the same mixture as above, and should also be allowed to set for at least twenty-four hours before removing the forms. It would be well to insert in the base, when casting, four pieces of ½-inch round or square steel reinforcing bars placed as indicated by the dotted lines in Fig. 95. These will add greatly to its strength, and will prevent it from cracking in case the foundation, upon which the pedestal is placed, is not perfectly true and level.

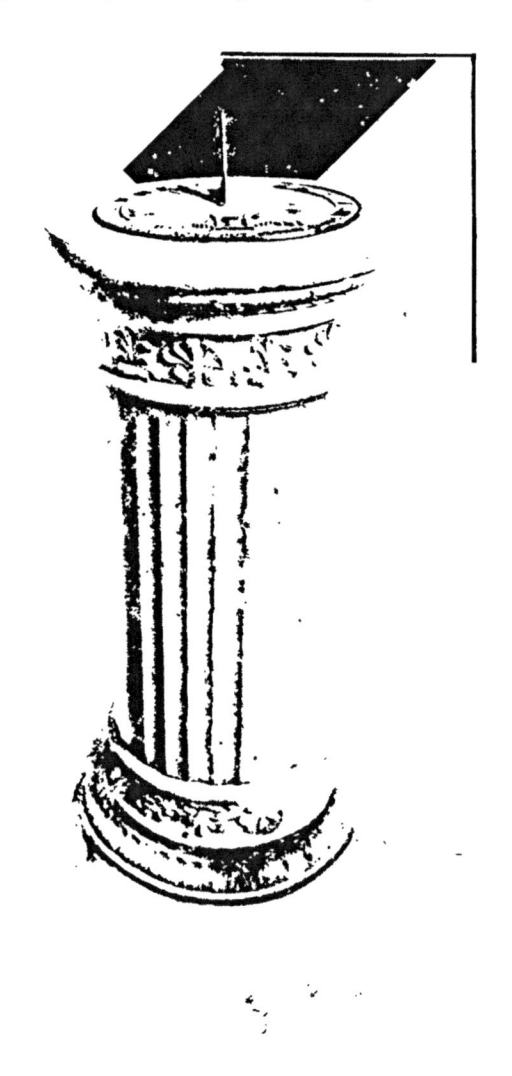

Fig. 104—Concrete Sun Dial Pedestal—Executed by J. C. Kraus

136 *Concrete Pottery and Garden Furniture*

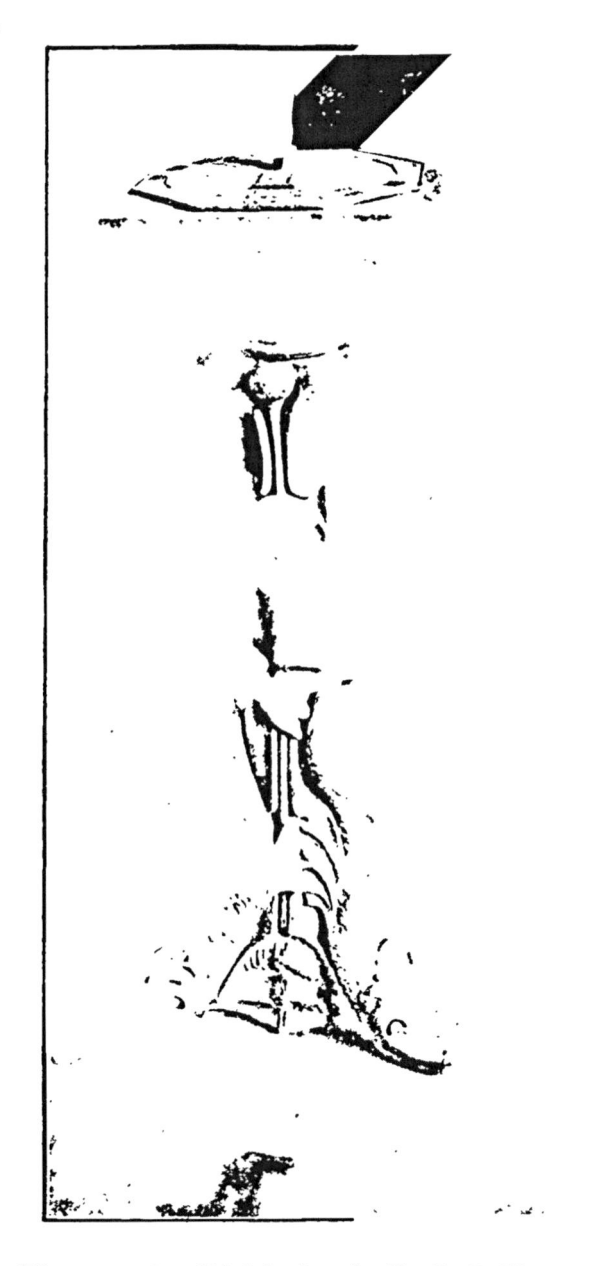

Fig. 105—Sun Dial Pedestal—By J. C. Kraus

If by any chance the casts should be injured, in removing them from the molds, they should be well wet down with water and pointed up with a mortar made of 1 part white Portland cement and 1 part of marble dust mixed with enough water to produce a fairly thick paste.

After having pointed up the various parts of the pedestal they should be allowed to stand for a short time, and then all of the pieces should be well soaked with water occasionally every day for at least ten days. This wetting down is known as the curing process, and it should be well attended to, as the hardness and durability of the product produced depend largely upon the care taken in properly curing the casts.

After the pieces have become thoroughly hardened or cured they can be assembled or set up in position, as shown in Figs. 93 and 94. The surfaces of the parts which are to be joined together should be sprinkled with water, and covered with a thin layer of cement mortar composed of 1 part of white Portland cement and 1 part of marble dust. They should be placed on each other, and worked around with a twisting motion until bedded in place. The surplus cement which is forced out at the joints should then be smoothed off, and the pieces allowed to set, without being disturbed, for from one to two days, in which time they will be firmly secured in place.

By using the mixture of white Portland cement and marble chips or screenings, as stated above,

138   Concrete Pottery and Garden Furniture

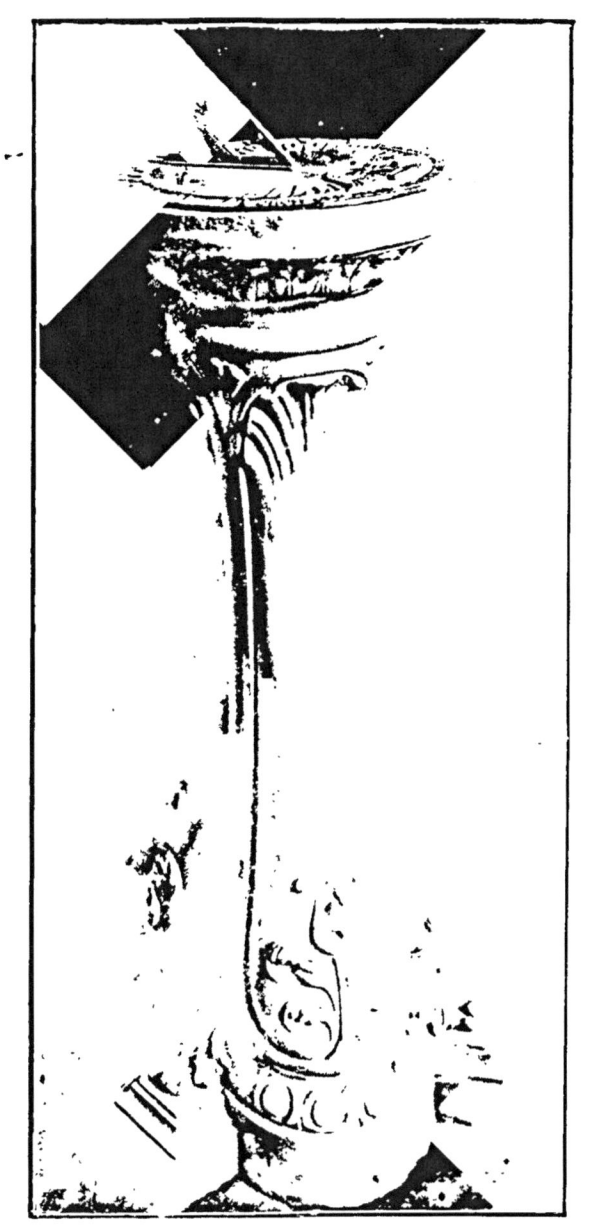

Fig. 106—Concrete Sun Dial or Vase Pedestal—Executed by J. C. Kraus

Concrete Pottery and Garden Furniture 139

the effect produced will resemble that of white marble. If one prefers the gray color of ordinary Portland cement, the mixture used should

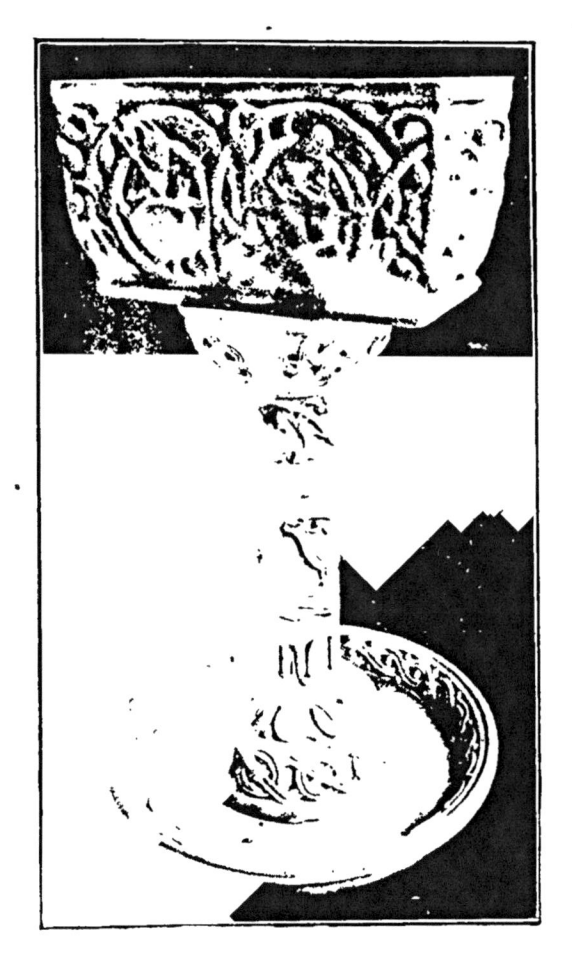

Fig. 107—Pedestal and Vase—By J. C. Kraut

then be composed of 1 part Portland cement to 2 parts of good clean sand and 2 parts of trap rock screenings or pebbles not to exceed ½ inch

140 *Concrete Pottery and Garden Furniture*

in size. If a sun dial is to be placed on the pedestal, it need not be cemented in place. They are

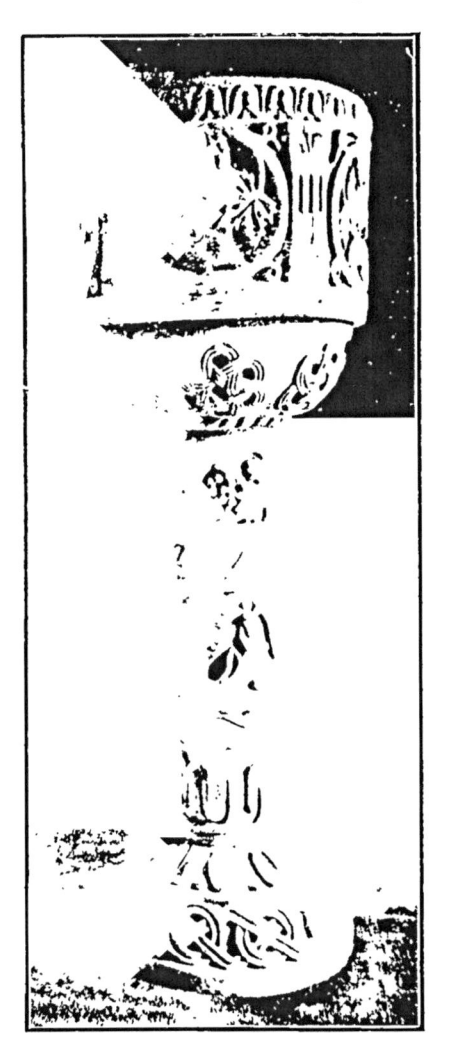

Fig. 108—Pedestal and Vase—By J. C. Kraus

usually made of brass or bronze, and their weight is sufficient to hold them down. When placing a

Concrete Pottery and Garden Furniture 141

sun dial, always see that its vane points to the north and that the pedestal is placed in the full rays of the sun. It would also be well to prepare a good solid foundation for the pedestal to rest

Fig. 109—Vases and Pedestals of Bold Design Lend Themselves Nicely to Concrete—Executed by Emerson & Norris Co.

on, for if this is not done it is apt to settle as the ground becomes soft in the spring time. In fact, all heavy garden furniture should be provided

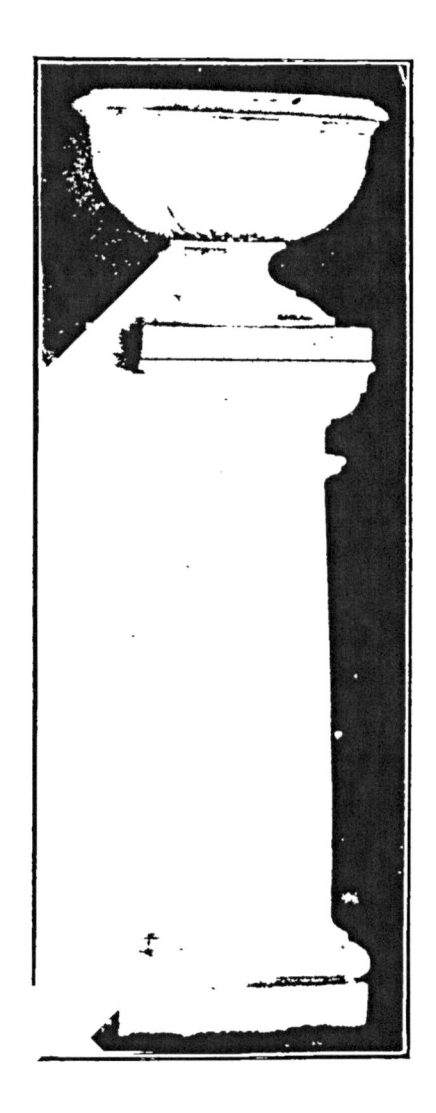

Fig. 110—Vase and Pedestal—Executed by Emerson & Norris Co.

with good solid foundations. These foundations should be from 2 to 3 feet deep, and in size should correspond to the size of the base of the piece which is to rest upon them. To prepare a foundation of this kind, all that is necessary is to dig a hole of the desired size and depth and to fill it with a mixture of 1 part Portland cement, 3 parts of sand, and 5 parts of broken stone or gravel. Add enough water to this to make it of the consistency of a thick pasty mass. Tamp it down well and level it off and allow it to set or harden for twenty-four hours, in which time the piece can be placed in position on it. In Fig. 103 is shown a pedestal of the same general lines as that shown in Fig. 93, the design, however, being somewhat elaborated. To produce a pedestal of this kind requires the incorporation of a plaster mold which is of a more complicated nature than the mold described above. Numerous other designs of pedestals are shown herewith, so as to give to the reader some idea of the wide possibilities in design which can be obtained with concrete.

CHAPTER XI.

CONCRETE BENCHES

The accompanying illustration, Fig. 111, shows a concrete bench which is especially designed with a view of meeting the demand for a simple yet artistic piece of lawn furniture, and at the same time can be made with a minimum amount of skill and expense by those who are as yet uninitiated in this work. A detail drawing of the

Fig. 111—A Simple Design for a Concrete Garden Bench—
Executed by the Author

end supports or the bench pedestals is shown in Fig. 112, and details of each piece used in the making of the wood mold for these end supports are shown in Fig. 113. The assembled mold ready for placing the concrete is shown in Figs. 115 and 116.

Concrete Pottery and Garden Furniture 145

The first thing to do is to procure a 1-inch board, 12 inches wide by 16 inches long, and cut it to the shape shown in Fig. 113 at *A*. This is to be used for the bottom of the mold, as shown in Fig. 115. Now cut another piece of board, also 1-inch thick, shaped as shown in Fig. 113 at *B*, and nail it down in its proper position on piece *A*.

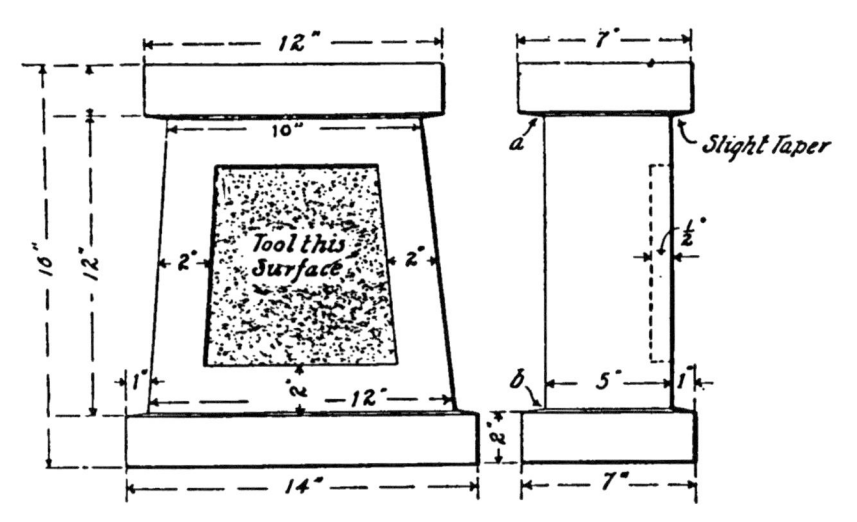

Fig. 112—Detail of Bench Pedestal

The next piece to make is piece *C* in Fig. 113. This piece forms the recessed panel; this panel as shown in Fig. 112 is only ½ inch deep, therefore this piece should be made of ½-inch board. Nail this securely in position, as shown in Fig. 115 on piece *B*. Be sure to bevel the edges of pieces *B* and *C*, as shown by the dotted lines in Fig. 115, for if this is not done, one will have trouble in releasing the mold from the concrete when it is set or hardened. Now proceed to make the pieces D, E, F, G, H, I, J, K, L, and M all of 1-inch thick material, care being taken to follow the dimensions given closely. When these pieces are

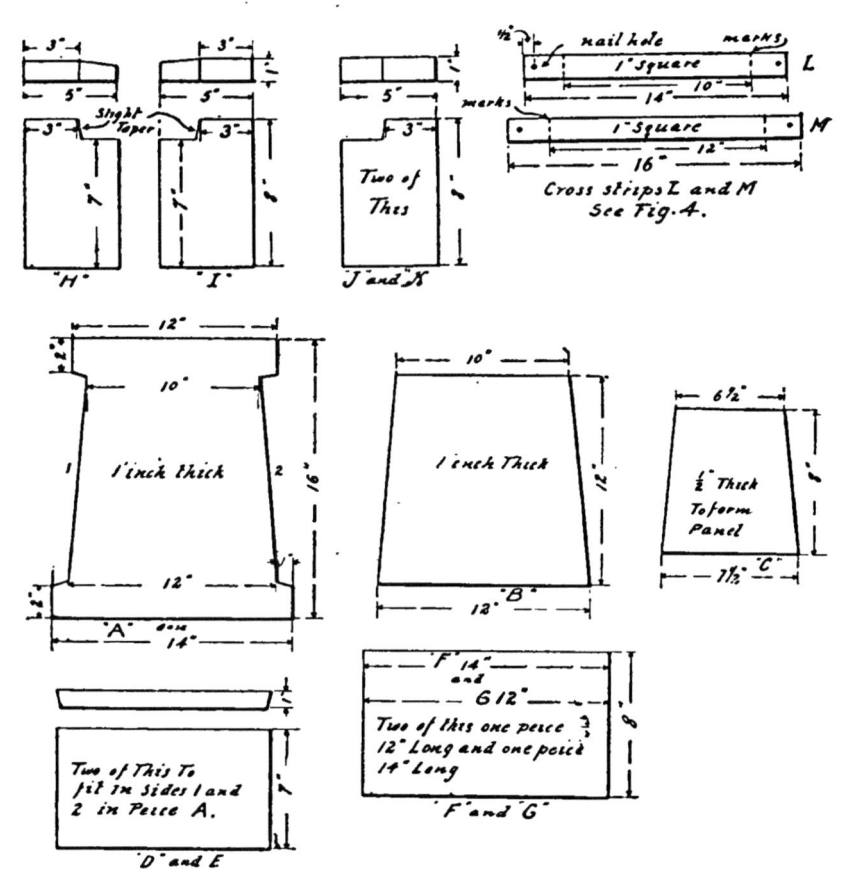

Fig. 113—Details of Mold for Bench Pedestal

all made, assemble them as shown in Fig. 115, using as few nails as possible in securing the pieces to one another; for when the concrete is hardened, the form or mold will have to be removed from

Concrete Pottery and Garden Furniture 147

it, and the fewer the nails used, the easier the form can be stripped from the cast. In making the form use green or unseasoned wood, as it is less liable to warp when the wet concrete mixture comes in contact with it. Before assembling the mold, each piece should be shellacked thoroughly

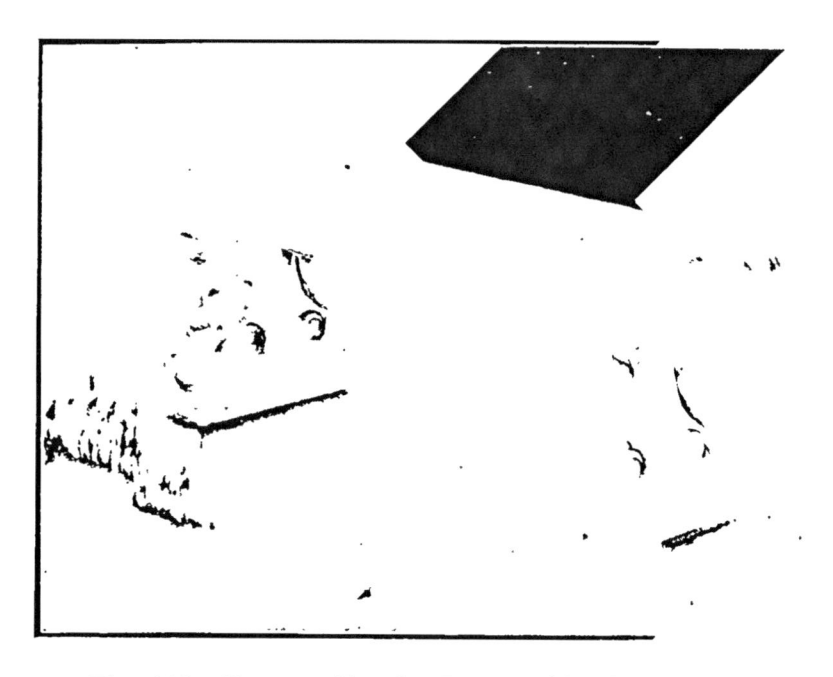

Fig. 114 – Concrete Bench – Executed by J. C. Kraus

on both sides as well as on the ends. This will in a great measure prevent the mold from absorbing moisture, and will thus prevent any tendency of the mold to warp or buckle. After having assembled the pieces, as shown in Figs. 115 and 116, if for any reason the joints do not match up as well as they might, they can be filled with putty or plaster of Paris, care being taken however to have everything square and true.

After having trued the mold up, the inside of it should again be shellacked, and when thoroughly dry, a thin coat of fairly thick oil should be given to all parts of the mold which will come in contact with the wet concrete. The mold is now ready to be filled with the concrete mixture, which should be composed of 1 part Portland cement, 2 parts of good clean sharp sand, and 2 parts of trap rock or pebbles ranging in size from ¼ inch to ½ inch. The method of mixing the concrete is as follows: It is important to follow the directions closely, for if the concrete is not properly mixed, an inferior product will be the result. First the sand should be evenly spread on a level water-tight platform. The cement should then be spread upon the sand. Then, after thoroughly mixing the cement and sand together until it is of a uniform color, water should be added, preferably by spraying, and the mass thoroughly turned over and over by means of a shovel or hoe until it is of a uniform consistency of a fairly thick putty. To this mortar should be added the stone or gravel, which has previously been drenched with water, and the whole mass should then be mixed or turned over until the aggregate or stone is thoroughly coated with mortar. An ordinary garden rake is a good tool with which to distribute the stones through the mortar, as it distributes them more uniformly than a shovel.

Concrete Pottery and Garden Furniture 149

The concrete thus mixed should be deposited in the form or mold as soon after mixing as possible. Under no conditions deposit concrete in molds which has been mixed more than two hours. To fill the mold use a shovel, care being taken to

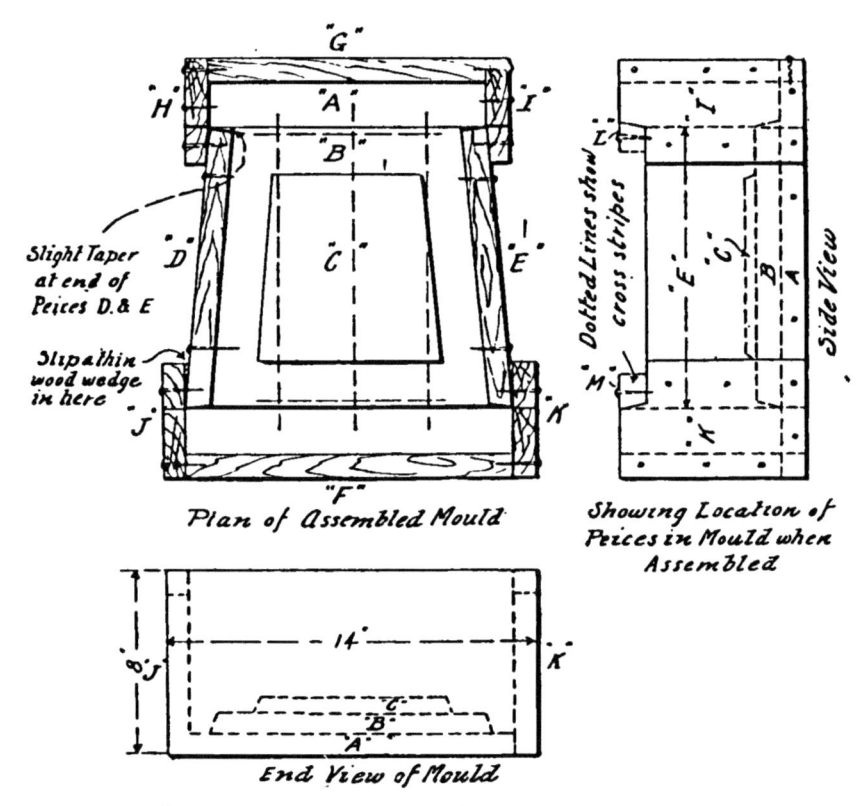

Fig. 115—Assembled Mold for Bench Pedestal

deposit the concrete into all of the corners. Tamp or tap it down well with the end of a piece of board. If the concrete has been properly mixed, this tamping will bring to the surface of the mass a slight skim of water. The mold should first

150 Concrete Pottery and Garden Furniture

be about half filled, and then a strip of Clinton wire cloth or other steel reinforcing fabric should be placed in the form, as shown by the dotted lines in the plan view of the assembled mold in Fig. 115. The proper size of wire cloth to use is that known as 3-inch by 12-inch mesh, made of Nos. 8 and 10 gage steel wire. If wire cloth is

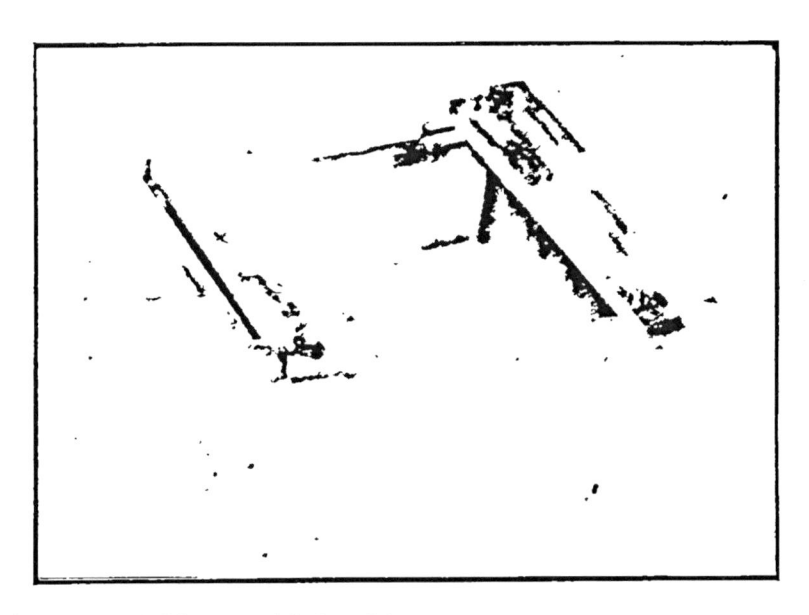

Fig. 116—Mold Assembled and in Position to Receive the Concrete

not available, any good No. 8 gage steel wire, cut and placed as shown, will answer the purpose. After having placed the reinforcing, continue to deposit the concrete, and tamp it down until it is level with the top of the sides D and E of the mold. Scrape or float this surface level, and then take the cross strips L and M, shown in Fig. 113, and secure them to the top of the mold and against the end pieces *H I* and *J K*, as shown by the dotted lines in the side elevation in Fig. 115. These cross pieces not only act as a form for the edges *a* and *b* of the pedestal, as shown in Fig. 112, but they also act as a brace to the sides of the form, and prevent them from spreading apart,

Fig. 117—Showing Interior of Mold for Bench Pedestal

due to the weight of the plastic concrete pushing against them.

After having secured these pieces in place, fill the portion of the mold thus formed flush with the top of the strips and the end pieces *G* and *F*. Tamp the concrete down, and smooth the surface off nicely. The filling of the mold is now complete, and it should not be disturbed for at least twenty-four hours, after which the cement should be wet down occasionally with a spray for at least a day. After having set or hardened for two days, the cast can be removed from the mold, and can be set aside to be cured or to harden up. This is done by sprinkling it with water two or three times a day for at least seven to ten days. Care should be taken when removing the mold not to injure it or the cast, as the mold if not broken can be used over and over again. In removing the mold from the cast, first detach the cross strips *L* and *M*, then the pieces *H*, *I*, *J*, and *K*, then the end pieces *F* and *G*, next the side pieces *E* and *D*, and then the bottom piece, composed of pieces *A*, *B*, and *C*. Before using the mold again, it should be thoroughly cleaned of any particles of cement which may have adhered to it. After having cleaned it well, oil the inside and proceed to assemble it as before, and cast the other pedestal for the bench in a similar manner as explained above.

The next step is to cast the slab or seat of the bench. This is 5 feet long by 18 inches wide by 3 inches thick. The form or mold for this is nothing more or less than an oblong box, having a bottom 5 feet long by 18 inches wide and four sides each 3 inches high, as shown in Fig. 118. The bench seat should be reinforced with the same size of wire cloth as was used in the pedestals, or by three ¼-inch round rods spaced 6 inches apart. The reinforcing steel should extend within 3 inches of all four sides, and should be placed about ½ inch from the under surface of the slab, as shown in Fig. 118.

It would be well to clearly mark the under surface of the slab, so as to know which surface the reinforcing is nearest to, after the slab is cast, as it is important when placing the slab on the pedes-

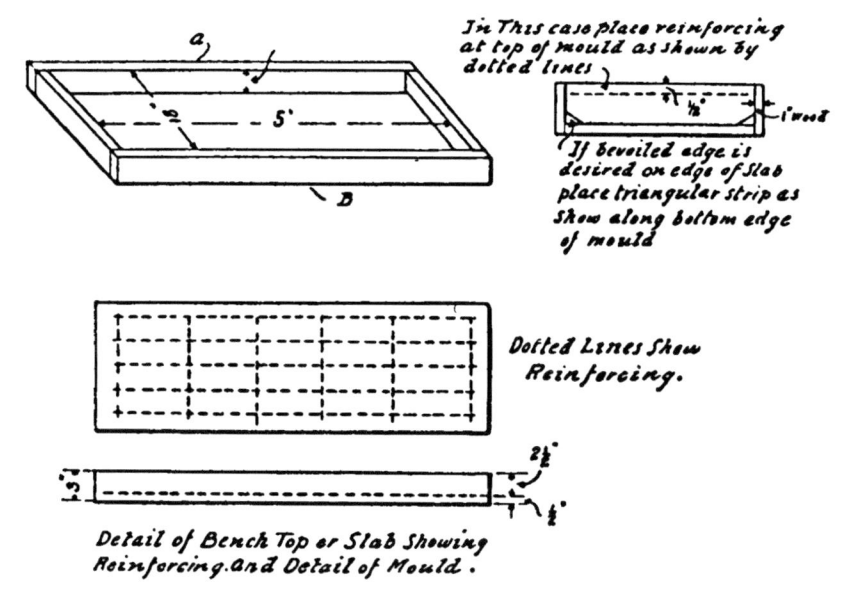

Fig. 118—Details of Bench Slab or Seat Showing Reinforcing and Mold for Same

tals to always have the reinforcing nearest the underside of the seat. Shellac and oil the inside of the mold, and proceed to fill it with a mixture composed of the same material as was used for the pedestals. First fill the mold to a depth of ½ inch, and then lay in the reinforcing as indicated in Fig. 118, and on top of this place the remaining

2½ inches of concrete and tamp it down well. This top surface will be the top of the finished bench seat, therefore it will pay to take pains in finishing it to as smooth a surface as one can. Cure or harden the slab in the same manner as described for curing the pedestals. It is well, however, not to attempt to remove the under part of the mold for at least from seven to ten days. The sides of the form can be removed any time after forty-eight hours.

A good smooth surface can be given to the bench by wetting it down well and rubbing it with a fairly fine grade of carborundum brick. By tooling the recessed panel in the outer sides of the pedestals by means of gently striking the surface with a chisel and hammer, a good stony effect will be produced, which will greatly add to the appearance of the ends.

If on taking off the mold the cast should in any way be injured, the damaged parts can readily be replaced or filled in by applying and forming into shape cement mortar composed of 1 part cement to 1 or 2 parts of sand. Before applying this mortar, be sure to wet down the surface of the cast thoroughly, for if not, trouble will be had in securing a good and permanent bond. In setting the bench up, place the pedestals about 7 inches in from the ends of the slab, as shown in the illustration.

It is unnecessary to secure the slab to the pedestals in any way, as its weight will keep it in place. If one should wish the top edges of the slab beveled off, a triangular strip of wood can be secured along the bottom edges of the mold, as shown in the cross section of the slab mold in Fig. 118.

By following along the same general directions as given for making the bench shown in Fig. 111, one may elaborate on the design of the bench ped-

Fig. 119—Design for Bench Pedestal with Curved Outline and Mold for Same

estals. For instance, in Fig. 119 is shown a pedestal having curved outlines. The mold for this is made similar to the mold shown in Fig. 115, with the exception of the sides. A simple way to make a form for a design of this kind is to use sheet tin or thin galvanized iron, as shown in Fig. 119. If one has not the facilities for cutting and bending the tin to shape, any tinsmith will do it for a trifling cost. All that is necessary to do in this case is to furnish the tinsmith with a full-sized drawing of the outline required and the width of the tin of which to make it. This width will be the same as the depth of the mold, and in no case need the depth of the mold be more than 7 inches. It is always well to brace these tin sides of the mold by means of strips of wood, as shown in Fig. 119. This will prevent them from bulging when the concrete mixture is placed in the mold.

Some very interesting surface effects can be obtained in the pedestals by using selected aggregates or stones. When using this method, the concrete is mixed exactly as previously explained, with the exception that instead of using plain pebbles or trap rock, one should use trap rock and white marble or broken-up red brick. The size of the pieces used should not exceed ½ inch to ¾ inch. Place the mixture in the mold as previously explained, but instead of allowing it to remain there for two days as before, remove the forms in from eighteen hours to twenty-four hours. The concrete will then be found a little soft. By spraying the cast with water and gently brushing the surface with a good stiff brush, the surface cement will be removed, and the stone and marble and pieces of red brick will gradually be exposed, thus producing a surface more or less resembling mosaic. The possibilities of the effects which can be obtained with this treatment, as pre-

Concrete Pottery and Garden Furniture 157

viously explained, are only limited by the colors and size of the stone aggregates which are available for use. If any surface cement should remain on the stones or exposed aggregate after the above treatment, a solution composed of 1 part commercial muriatic acid to 4 parts of water can be applied to the surface of the cast by means of a

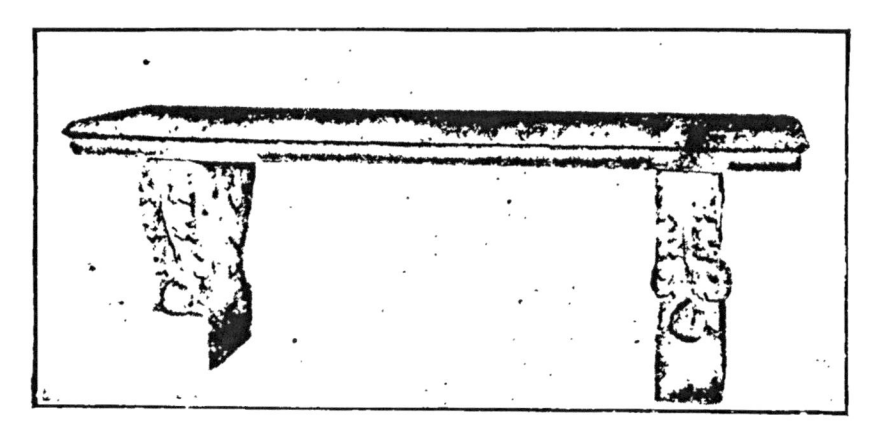

Fig. 120—Ornate Concrete Bench—Executed by the Erkins Studios

brush. This solution should be allowed to remain on the surface for from fifteen to twenty minutes. Then the surface should be thoroughly cleaned off by means of washing with good clean water and a stiff brush. This acid treatment will cut away all surplus cement and will leave all of the stones clean and bright, thus producing a surface full of life and sparkle.

CHAPTER XII.

CONCRETE FENCES

Concrete fences are becoming more in favor every year, for the reason that they always look substantial and neat, and at the same time require practically no expense for maintenance.

The accompanying illustrations are suggestive of what is and can be done in concrete fence work.

Foundations

The first thing to do in building a fence is to prepare a good foundation or base for it to rest

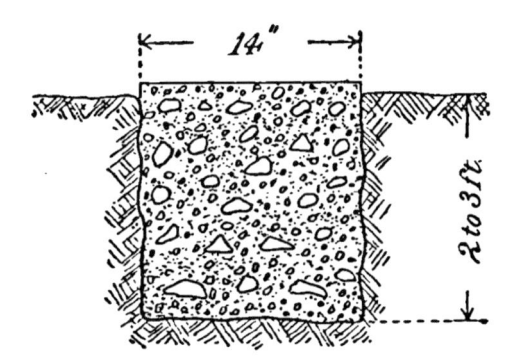

Fig. 121 — Detail of Concrete Foundation

on. Care should always be taken to see that the base is placed deep enough in the ground to obviate all trouble which may arise from frost or the heaving of the ground in the spring of the year. The depth of the foundation depends largely upon locality and the nature of the soil, but usually a depth of from 18 inches to 3 feet from the surface of the ground is sufficient to overcome any trouble from frost.

To prepare the foundation, a trench should first be dug, as shown in Fig. 121. This should be about 14 inches wide. The depth depends, as stated above, upon the locality and nature of the soil. The bottom of the trench should be well tamped down, so as to make a good solid bottom on which to deposit the concrete which should be composed of 1 part Portland cement, 3 parts of sand, and 5 parts of broken stone or gravel. This mixture should be placed while fairly wet, and should be well tamped down and leveled off. The foundation after having set or hardened for from one to three days will be ready to receive the fence posts and rails or panels which may be of various designs.

Fence Posts

The fence posts are usually made in wooden molds, and set up and cemented in place on the foundation after they are finished. The posts and post caps are cast separately, as shown in Figs. 122 and 123. A detail of the post mold is shown in Fig. 122. It consists, as shown, of a square box built up of 1-inch boards. These posts can be made of any desired dimensions. As a rule, a good size is about 12 inches square by from 3 feet to 4 feet high. A mixture composed of 1 part Portland cement, 2 parts of sand, and 4 parts of broken stone or gravel should be used for making the posts.

The post mold should be placed on end, as shown in Fig. 122, and the concrete should be de-

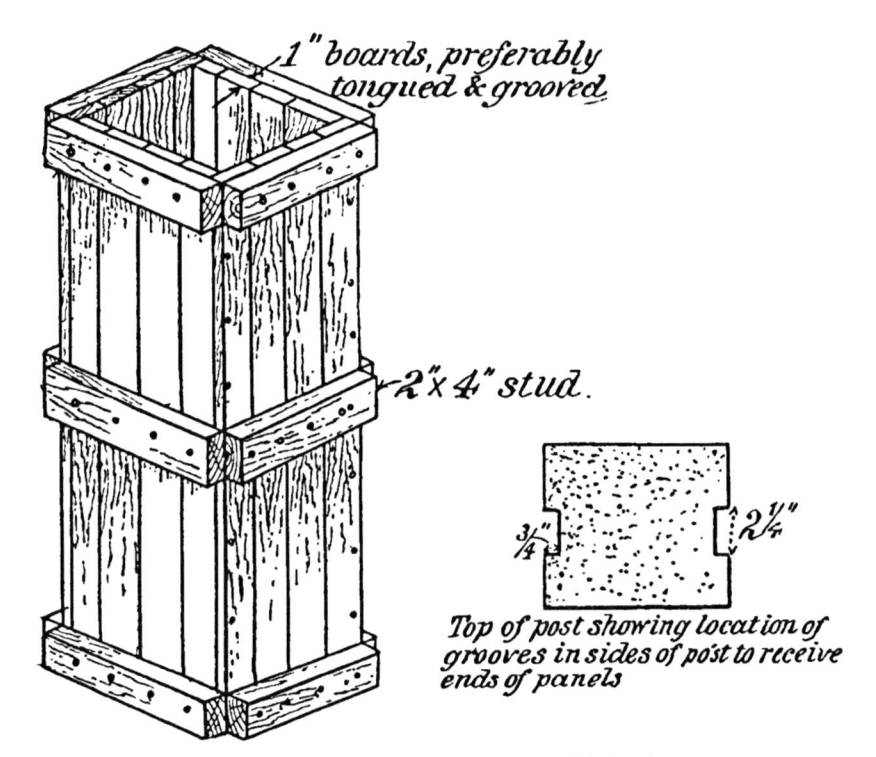

Fig. 122—Detail of Wooden Mold for Posts

posited while in a pasty state. It should be well tamped down, and by working the heavy stone away from the sides of the mold, while depositing, by means of a wooden paddle or pitchfork, thus allowing the finer particles of cement and sand to come to the face of the mold a smooth surface will be obtained on the cast. It would be well to shellac and grease the mold before depositing the concrete. Be sure to get the top and bottom of the mold square with the sides, for if this is not done, more or less trouble will be had in truing the posts up when placing them in position on the base or foundation.

Post Caps

The caps as stated above are cast separately from the posts. A simple form or mold for the post caps can be made as shown in Fig. 123. This is composed of a wooden box made to the desired

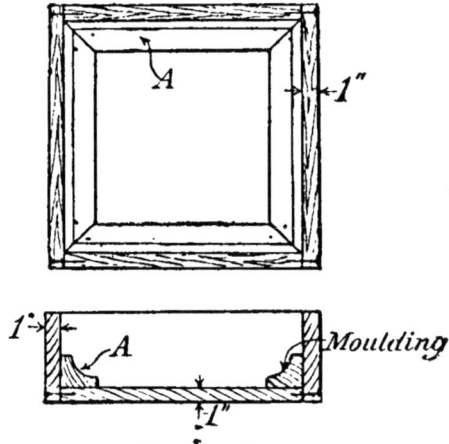

Fig. 123—Detail of Mold for Fence Post Cap

dimensions of the finished cap. The bottom or curved portion of the cap, shown at *A*, can be produced by securing to the inside bottom edges of the mold strips of wood molding of any desired shape neatly mitered at the corners as shown. This molding comes in standard sizes and shapes, and can be procured in long strips at almost any carpenter's shop. Shellac and oil the inside of this mold well before placing the concrete, for if one neglects to do this, trouble will be had in stripping the mold from the cast. When stripping or removing the mold from the cast, remove all four sides first before attempting to remove the bottom. It will be noted that the molding is secured to the bottom of the mold only, the four sides merely resting snugly against it when the mold is assembled. Care should also be taken to level off and trowel smoothly the top of the cap after the concrete is placed in the mold. Use the same mixture for casting these caps as was used in making the posts.

Fence Panels—Lattice Design

Various designs are resorted to in filling in between the posts in fence work, such as balasters, scroll designs, panels, etc. The diamond or lattice design of railing or panel, shown in Fig. 124, is largely used for porch work as well as fences. It is cast in one piece and is reinforced with a sheet of 6-inch mesh No. 4 expanded metal placed in the center of the concrete strands which are made about 2 inches square. The expanded metal reinforcing lends itself nicely to this design, inasmuch as the meshes are of a diamond shape. If, however, this metal is not available, $\frac{1}{8}$-inch round or square steel rods can be used for reinforcing the panel, with good results. The method of making a fence panel of this kind is simple. All that is required in the way of a form is a box 2 inches deep by the desired height and length of the panel which is to be made. In the bottom of this box locate the position of the diamond-shaped holes. Then make of wood as many diamond-

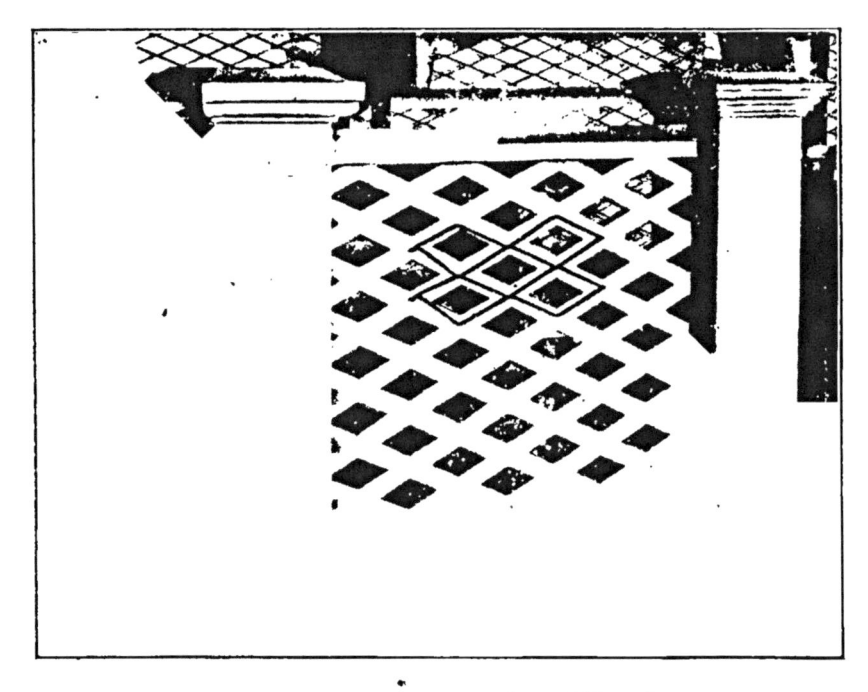

Fig. 124—Lattice Design of Panel

shaped blocks as are required, and secure them by nails in their proper position to the bottom of the mold. Allow a good draft or taper on all sides of the blocks as shown, so that the fence panel when cast can be easily withdrawn from the mold. Before casting, shellac and oil well all parts of the mold that will come in contact with the wet concrete. When the mold is complete, as shown in Fig. 125, place about 1 inch of concrete in it, then place the sheet of expanded metal or steel rods in position on it, and proceed to fill the mold flush with the top. Level off the concrete and allow it to set for two or three days, occasionally wetting it down well with water. After the concrete is hardened, the mold can easily be removed by gently tapping the surface of the exposed diamond

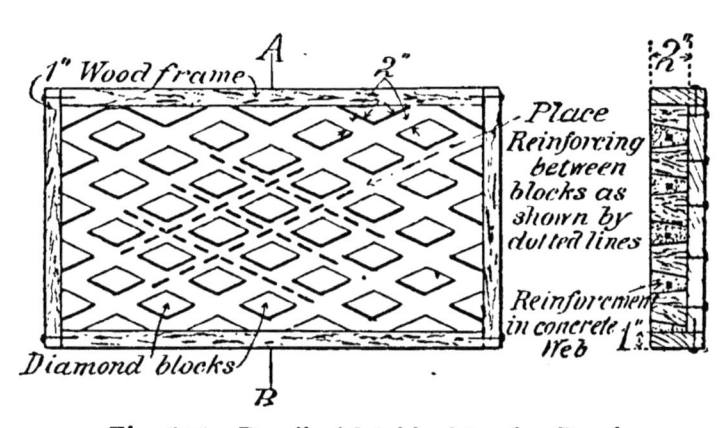

Fig. 125—Detail of Mold of Lattice Panel

blocks here and there throughout surface of the mold. Any corners of the cast that may have been broken or injured in removing the cast from the mold can be readily pointed up with a mixture of cement mortar composed of 1 part Portland cement to 2 parts of sand. The whole surface of the panel can then be well wet down and painted with a mixture of neat cement and water mixed to the consistency of a thick cream; this on drying out will produce a good uniform color to the whole piece. The concrete mixture used in making this panel should be composed of 1 part Portland cement, 2 parts of sand, and 2 parts of gravel or broken stone, not to exceed ¼ inch in size.

In setting this panel in place, the fence posts

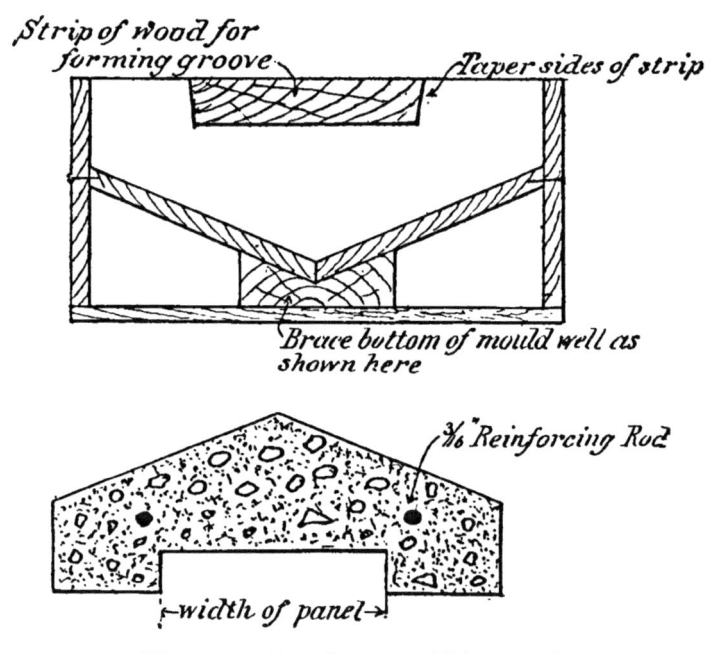

Fig. 126—Detail of Mold for Coping

should be provided with a groove 2⅛ inches to 2¼ inches wide by ½ inch to ¾ inch deep in the middle of their two opposite sides, as shown in Fig. 122. This is to allow of the ends of the panels to set into the posts. After having located the panel in its proper position in the groove or recess, the recess should be filled in with cement mortar flush with the face of the post, thus producing a good smooth finish as well as firmly cementing the panel in place.

Copings

The panels should be topped off with a coping, as shown in Fig. 124. The underside of this coping should also be provided with a groove, as shown in Fig. 126, of the same dimensions as the grooves in the sides of the posts, so that it can be let down on and securely cemented to the top of the panel. This coping can be cast in a wooden mold made as shown in Fig. 126. A strip of wood, tapered on the sides as shown, can be used to form the groove in the bottom of the coping. The mold should first be filled to within the thickness of this strip from its top. The strip should then be centered, and the concrete filled in on both sides of it until flush with the top of the mold. A mixture composed of 1 part Portland cement to 3 parts of sand and fine gravel will give good results for this class of work.

Rubble Panel

Another very effective panel for fences is the rubble panel made of field stone shown in Fig. 127. This is made in a mold composed of four pieces of 2-inch by 4-inch lumber. This frame is made of the desired size of the finished panel. It is then laid down flat on a good level piece of ground and filled in with about 1 inch of cement mortar composed of 1 part Portland cement and 3 parts of sand. A sheet of steel reinforcing mesh such as expanded metal or steel rods is then placed on top of this 1 inch of mortar, and over the reinforcing is deposited about 2 inches more of the cement mortar, into which the field stones are embedded.

Fig. 127—Rubble Panel

The stones before embedding into the mortar should be well wet down. This panel should be allowed to harden, before attempting to raise it from its position, for at least from four to six days. It should also be occasionally well sprinkled with water. After it has thoroughly hardened it can be set up in place between the fence posts in a similar manner as explained for setting up the diamond design of panel. After this panel has been set in place, the rough side of it can be cleaned off and well wet down and finished, by means of plastering it with a cement mortar made of 1 part Portland cement to from 2 to 3 parts of sand.

Solid Rubble Wall

The same rubble effect can be obtained in a solid wall by building up on the foundation a wooden mold, as shown in Fig. 128. This mold should then be filled in with heavy and light field stone, and when the mold is filled level with the top, a fairly thin creamy mixture of 1 part Portland cement to 2 parts of sand can be poured into the mold. This cement grout as it is called will find its way into all of the crevices or voids between the stones, and will securely cement them together. The mold should be removed in from twelve to twenty-four hours at the longest. The surface of the wall should then be scrubbed down well with a good stiff wire brush and plenty of water. This treatment will remove all of the surface cement, and thus expose the stone to view. If desired, a coping can then be cemented to the top of the wall, as shown in Fig. 127. A wall of this kind can be made of any length. Fence posts can then be cast

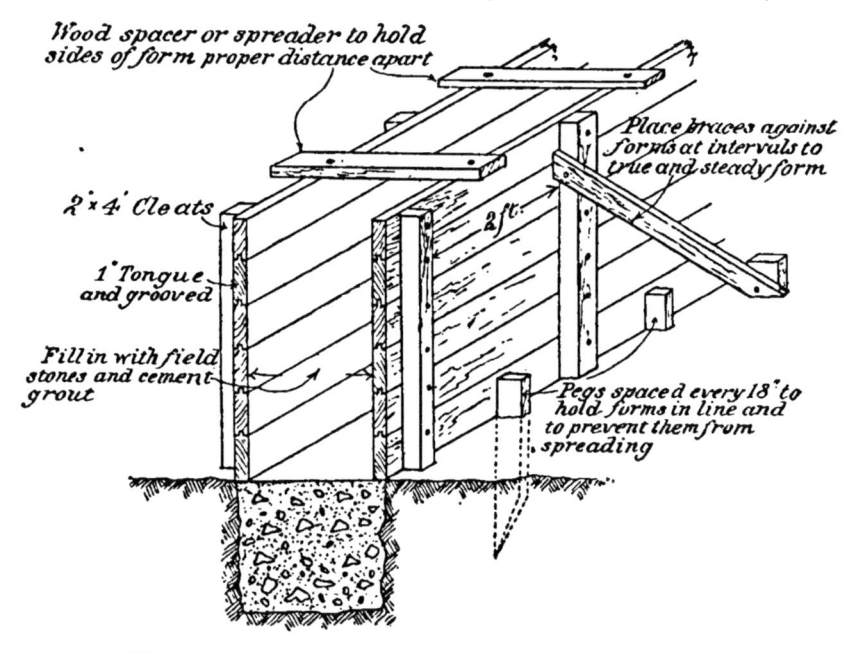

Fig. 128—Detail of Mold for Solid Rubble Wall

in place at the ends, or they can be cast separately, as previously explained and set up in place.

Assembling Panel Fences

As stated above, when panels are used in the construction of a fence, the posts should always be cast with a groove or recess for them to fit into. When assembling a panel fence, the first post should be firmly cemented in position on the foundation or base with a mixture of cement mortar composed of 1 part Portland cement to 2 parts of sand. One end of the panel should then be located in the groove in the fence post, and should be temporarily held in position until the next post is moved up into place, so as to engage the other end of the panel in the groove cast in its side. The second post and the panel should then be trued up and held in position by wooden wedges. The whole then should be firmly cemented in place with cement mortar, and the remaining posts and panels set up in like manner on the foundation until the fence is complete.

Low Cement Copings

Low cement copings, such as shown in Fig. 129, are much in vogue along the sides of paths as well as sometimes being used to indicate the dividing line between two pieces of property. These copings can be easily constructed by the use of two boards, a few wooden pegs, and a metal template cut to the desired outline of the top of the finished coping. The first thing to do is to set the boards up along the foundation or base, as shown in Fig. 130, which has previously been made to the desired width, then drive in the wooden pegs as shown, spacing them about 16 inches apart. Nail the side boards to them firmly, and then line up the sides and level off the top of the boards. Now fill in the space between the boards with a mixture of 1 part Portland cement and 4 parts of fairly coarse sand.

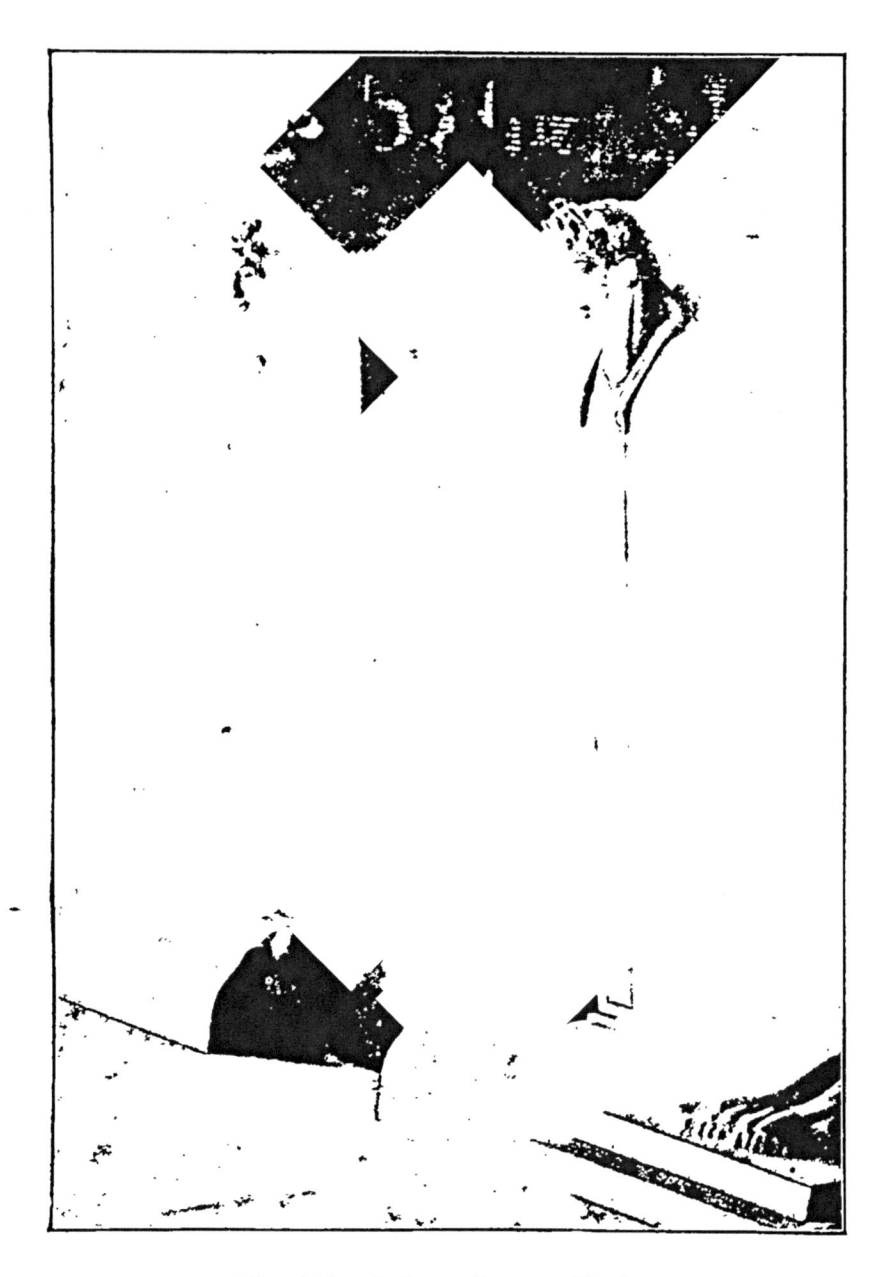

Fig. 129—A Low Cement Coping

172   Concrete Pottery and Garden Furniture

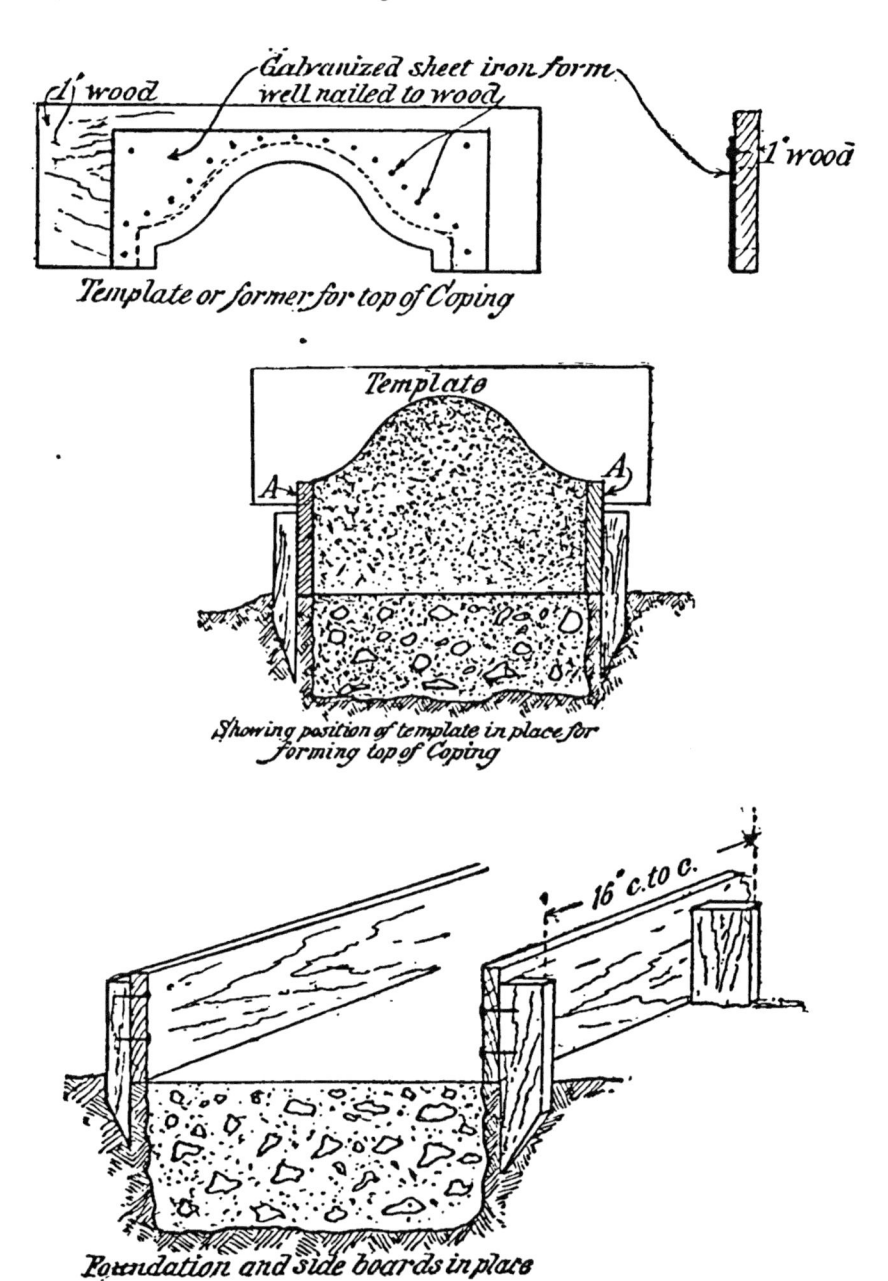

Fig. 130 — Detail of Mold, Template, etc., for Low Coping

Do not make this mixture too wet. Now make a former or template out of a heavy piece of tin or galvanized iron. Cut this to the form of the desired shape of the top of the coping, and nail it securely to a piece of 1-inch board as shown in the illustration. Place this in position on the top of the two side boards, letting the edges of it lap over the sides of the boards, as shown at *A*.

Now on the cement already placed between the side boards build up more of the mixture until it reaches high enough to be scraped or cut off by the template as it is moved back and forth over the top of the side boards. Keep adding cement to the top of the coping and packing it down, at the same time moving the template back and forth until a good smooth even surface is obtained of the same outline as the cut-out portion of the template or former.

With this method a coping of any desired shape and length can be made at a small expense.

Balustrades

Probably one of the oldest designs of fence, and one that is still popular for certain architectural effects, is the balustrade. This is made up of a number of small pillars set on a base and topped off with a coping, as indicated in the half-tone illustration, Fig. 131. Formerly these balustrades were made of stone or marble, and were used only in the highest class of work, owing to their great cost, due to the fact that each baluster had to be

174 *Concrete Pottery and Garden Furniture*

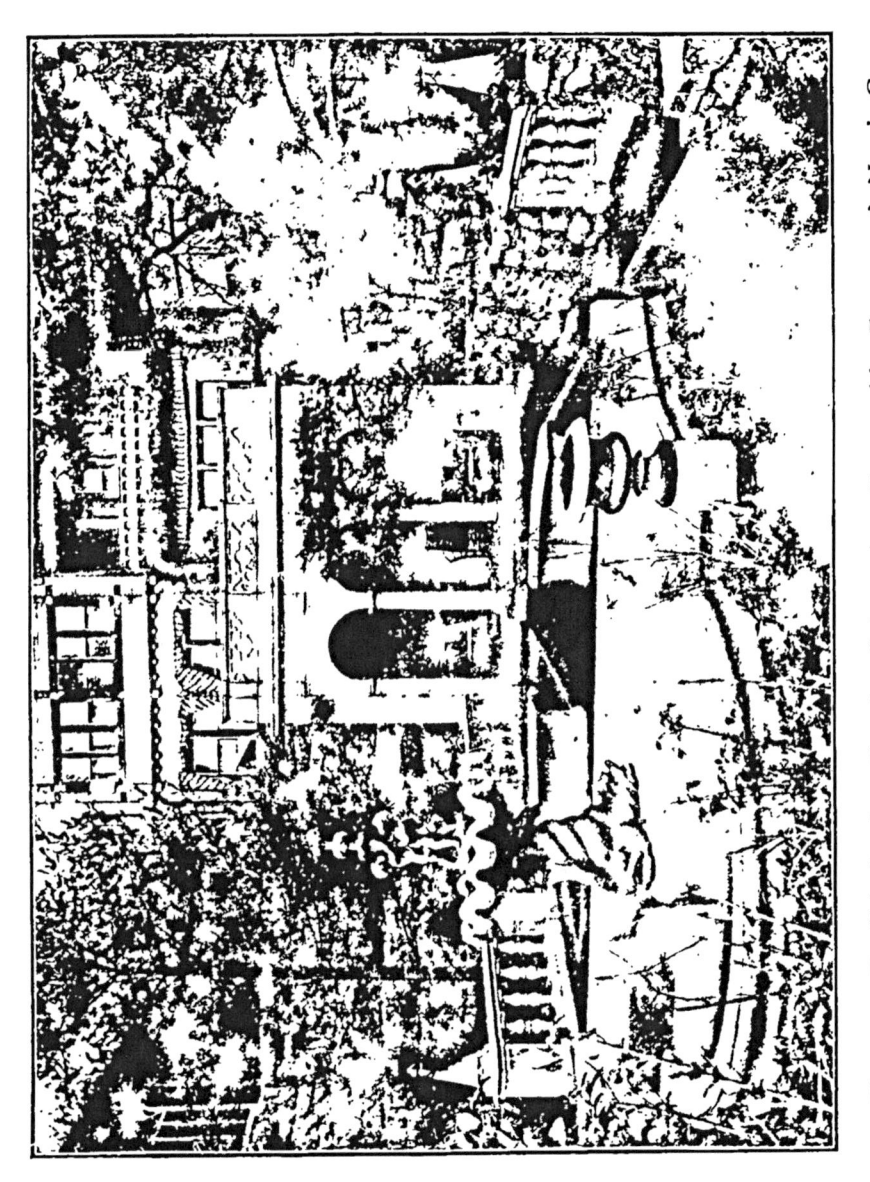

Fig. 131—English Garden, Showing Balustrades—Executed by Emerson & Norris Co.

Concrete Pottery and Garden Furniture 175

cut out of a solid block or piece of stone. These balustrades are now made of concrete, and are used in places where formerly, owing to their expense, their use was prohibitive. The half-tone illustrations shown in Figs. 132, 133, 134, 135, and 136 show different views of the

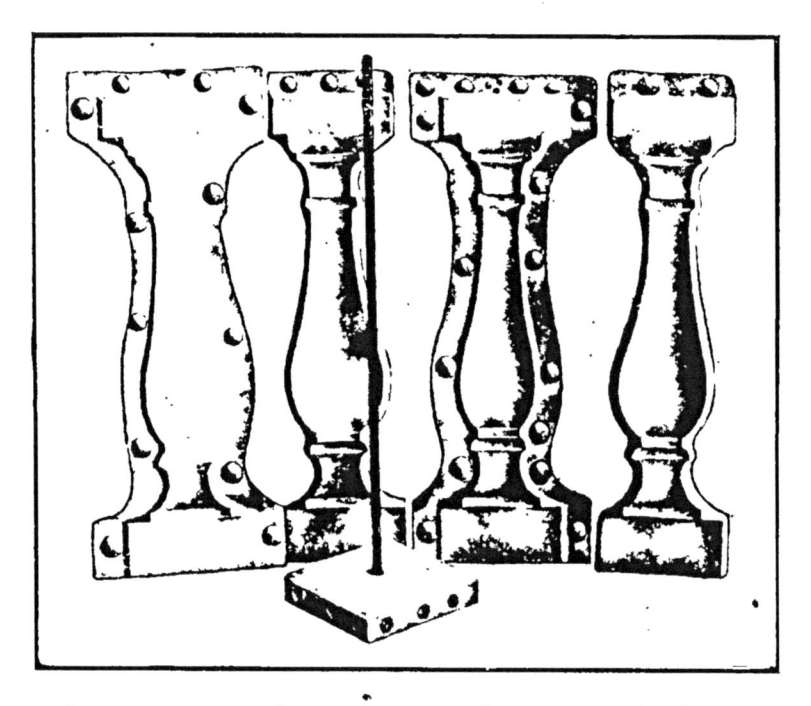

Fig. 132—Four Sides and Base of Plaster Mold for Baluster

plaster mold in which the balusters are cast, as well as the various steps in the making of a concrete baluster. The first thing to do in order to make the mold for a concrete baluster is to procure a model. This can be of either wood, plaster, or stone, or it can be modeled in clay.

Perhaps the cheapest way would be to procure from a carpenter or builder a stock model of a wood baluster of pleasing design. This should be well coated with two or three coats of shellac.

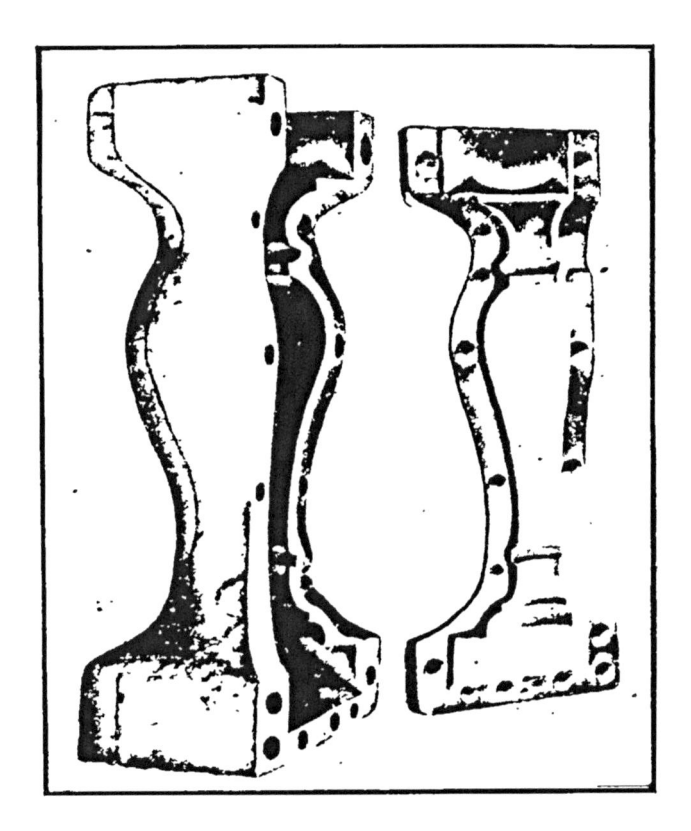

Fig. 133—Showing Baluster Mold Assembled with One Side Off

It should then be oiled and placed on the working bench, as shown in Fig. 137. A square block of plaster A, 1 inch to 1½ inches in thickness, to correspond in size and shape to the base B of the baluster, should then be made.

Fig. 134—Baluster Mold Assembled and Being Filled with the Concrete Mixture

178   Concrete Pottery and Garden Furniture

This should be placed and secured to the end of the baluster at *B* as indicated. Now take some modelers' clay, and place it along the entire length of the baluster from *C* to *D,* as indicated by the

Fig. 135—Stripping the Mold from the Concrete Cast

shaded portions *E* and *F* in the end view No. 1. Smooth off the surfaces *G* and *H* of the clay to an angle of about 45 degrees. After having prepared the clay on the model of the baluster as described above, block up the two ends by placing

Fig. 136—Pointing Up the Baluster

180   Concrete Pottery and Garden Furniture

against them two pieces of board, as shown at *I* and *J*. Now get a fairly large tin dishpan and

Fig. 137.—Progressive Steps in the Making of a Plaster Mold for a Baluster

partly fill it with water, and to this add plaster of Paris, at the same time stirring it well, until the mixture is of the consistency of thick cream. Pour this mixture over the model of the baluster and into the cavity formed by the clay strips and the two end boards. Allow the plaster to set or harden for about ten minutes, after which time the clay and end boards can be removed. Now turn the model over, letting it rest on the plaster shell just cast, as shown in the end view No. 2. Then proceed as before to cast a plaster shell on side K of the model, using the clay sides and end boards. After the plaster has hardened, remove the clay and boards and turn the model over into the position indicated in the end view No. 3. Cut joggle holes in to the angular faces of the plaster shell as indicated in the various half-tone illustrations, then shellac and oil these surfaces well. Now proceed to cast section L of the plaster mold. After this is hardened, turn the model over again and cast section N of the mold, as shown in end view No. 4. Let this harden for from ten to fifteen minutes. Now if the angular edges of the plaster have been properly oiled as directed, a slight tapping here and there on the plaster shell will be sufficient to release it from the model of the baluster. The inside of the plaster mold should now be cleaned up and be given two coats of shellac. After drying it should be well oiled with a fairly thick oil to prevent the cement when casting from adhering to it. Before assembling the various parts of the mold, a hole should be made in the center of the piece A. This hole should be about ½ inch deep and large enough to receive the end of a ½-inch round steel rod. Each baluster should be cast with a rod of this size running through it, from end to end. This rod not only acts as a reinforcing for the baluster, but it also helps to hold them firmly in place when setting them up in the balustrade. Now assemble the various parts of the plaster mold, and secure them firmly together by irons shaped as shown in the half-tone illustrations, Figs. 134 and 135. To cast the baluster, set the mold on end as shown in Fig. 134, and fill it with a mixture of 1 part Portland cement, 2 parts of sand, and 3 parts of broken stone or gravel not to exceed ¼ inch in size. Mix these all together thoroughly, while dry, and then add enough water to this mixture to make it of a creamy consistency, so that it can be poured into the mold from a pail as shown. After pouring let the mold set on end, undisturbed, for about twenty-four hours. At the end of this time the concrete will be hard enough to allow of the removal of the mold.

Before casting the next baluster, clean and oil the inside of the mold well. If any part of the baluster should have been injured in removing the mold, it can be readily pointed up with a cement mortar made of 1 part Portland cement to 2 parts of sand. Wet the injured portion well before starting to point it up, for if this is not done, trouble will he had in getting the mortar to adhere to the baluster.

The base upon which to set the balusters can

be made in a similar manner as described for the making of the low coping, previously explained; but instead of having a curved outline to the top, the base upon which to set the balusters should be made flat. Holes can be made at proper intervals in the top of the base, to receive the $\frac{1}{2}$-inch rods which are cast in the balusters, while the cement is still in a soft state. This will facilitate matters when setting up the balustrade. The coping can be cast in a square wooden mold in any lengths desired in a similar manner as described for the casting of the coping for the lattice panel explained above. In setting up the balustrade wet all parts which are to be cemented together, and use a cement mortar composed of 1 part Portland cement to 2 parts of sand.

Combination Metal Frame and Cement Mortar Fence

This type of fence is used where a good, neat, strong, and permanent structure is desired. Its life is practically unlimited, and the cost for maintenance, when properly built, is nothing. No molds or wooden forms are required in its construction. It is made up on a steel skeleton covered with metal lath. In the fence here illustrated expanded metal lath was used. A detail of the steel skeleton or framework is shown in Fig. 138, and in Fig. 139 is shown the progressive operations in the building of the structure. Fig. 140 shows the fence as it appears when completed.

184 Concrete Pottery and Garden Furniture

On referring to Fig. 138, a clear idea of how the framework is assembled will be obtained. The posts are made of 3-inch steel I beams, and are firmly imbedded in a foundation of concrete 15 inches square by 3 feet deep. As shown they are

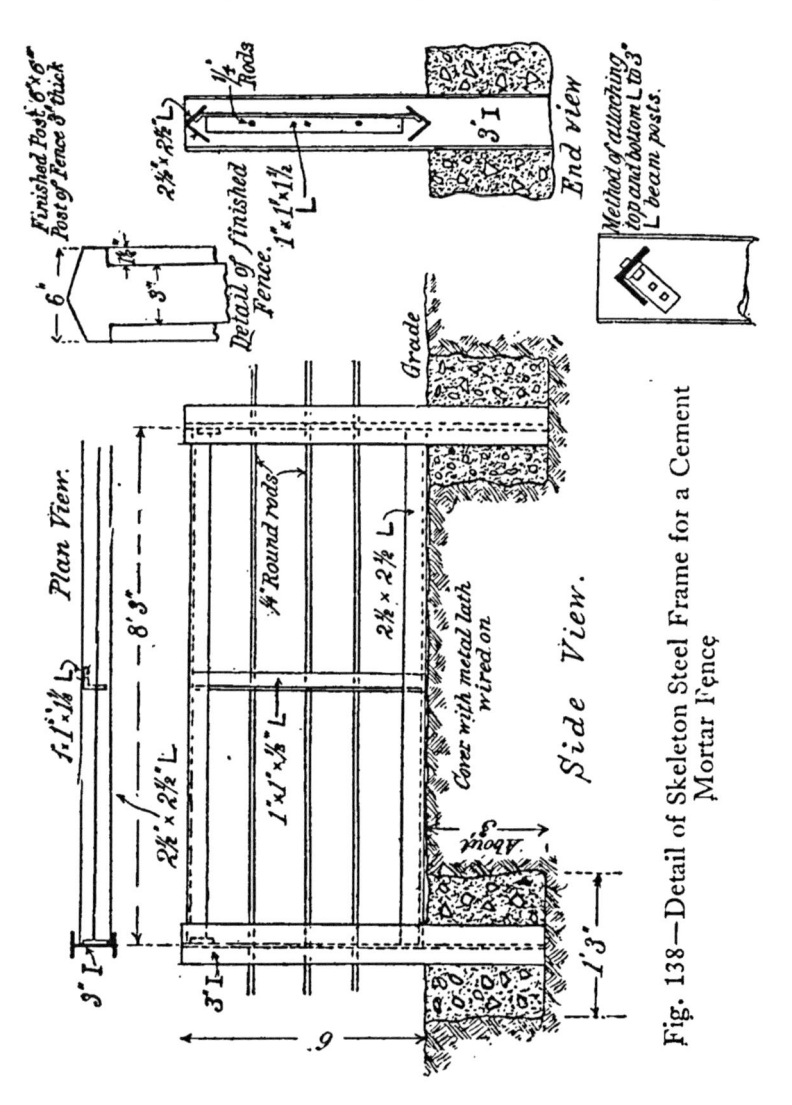

Fig. 138—Detail of Skeleton Steel Frame for a Cement Mortar Fence

placed at 8 feet 3 inches centers, and the total height of the posts from the bottom of the foundation to their tops is 9 feet. The top and bottom rails are made of 2½-inch x 2½-inch steel angles. It will be noticed that the bottom rail is placed with the point of the angle down. The object of this is to relieve the fence, to a large extent, from the upward pressure due to the rising

Fig. 139—Progressive Operations in the Making of a Cement Mortar Fence

of the ground in the Spring time. If the bottom was left flat as is usually done, a direct pressure would come on it, but by forming it as shown the tendency, when the ground rises, is for it to slide off on each side; thus relieving the fence of the direct pressure which it would otherwise be subjected to.

Midway between the posts are secured to the top and bottom rail 1-inch x 1-inch x ⅛-inch angles, and in the center of these angles, as well as in the webs of the I beams used for the posts, are provided three ⅜-inch holes, through which are inserted three ¼-inch round steel rods.

After this framework is set up, metal lath is wired to it. as shown in Fig. 139, and the steel

Fig. 140—Cement Mortar Fence Complete

skeleton is then complete and is ready for the application of the cement mortar.

The first coat of cement mortar should be made up of 1 part Portland cement to 2 or 3 parts of fairly coarse sand, and should contain a sufficient amount of long cow or goat hair to form a good key. The first coat should be applied to the thickness of about 1 inch, and its face should be well scratched to make a good key for the second coat to bond to. After this coat has been applied to one side of the lath and has become hard, the reverse side of the fence, the surface of which will appear very rough, should first be thoroughly saturated with water and then be plastered, to a like thickness, with a mortar of the same composition, except that the hair should be omitted. The posts should be treated with mortar in the same manner as the panels, forming them into shape as the work progresses. The finishing coat can now be applied to both sides. The cement mortar for the finish should be of the same proportion as used for the first coat; but before applying it, be sure to saturate the first coat with water, for if this is not done, a good bond between the first and finish coat will not be obtained. The top of the fence can be finished off square or a coping can be placed on it, as fancy dictates. If a coping is desired, it can be cast separately and set in place, or it can be run in place in a similar manner as previously explained for making a low coping.

The surface of the fence can be finished with any one of the artistic surfaces which are possible to obtain with this material, such as a rough or smooth surface, slap dash, pebble dash, or rough cast. Even some color can be incorporated if so desired. The dimensions for the framework as well as the construction of the frame as given in Fig. 138 are of a specific case, and are given more as a suggestion as to what can be done along these lines rather than to follow in detail.

The general principles given for the construction of this type of fence can be modified to suit any size or shape of fence demanded by the various conditions that may arise.

CHAPTER XIII.

MISCELLANEOUS

Tools

Aside from the tools described and illustrated throughout the various chapters, which can be made as the work progresses, one will require one or more of the tools here mentioned, depending upon the class of work which is to be undertaken.

Pointing tools, steel float, wood float, rake, wire brush, scrubbing brush, trowels, straight edges, hoe, shovel, nippers (for cutting wire), chisel (for cutting steel bars), shears (for cutting sheet metal), hand saw, wood plane, screw driver, hammer and a mixing box.

Reinforcing

There are innumerable types of reinforcing materials on the market. To describe them all would take up too much space; therefore the author will here only call attention to the necessity of using reinforcing, and give a few brief remarks as to why it is used. As the term implies, reinforcing is used to strengthen or reinforce the various objects made of concrete. When reinforcing is used in concrete, the product becomes a combination of steel and concrete and is known as "reinforced concrete." Reinforcing is made of steel, and the types which are most used for reinforcing the class of work described in the foregoing pages are in the forms of metal lath and of round or square steel rods. Concrete like all other materials expands and contracts under temperature changes; therefore, concrete articles of any size must be well reinforced, not only to give them additional strength with which to withstand handling, etc., but also to prevent them from cracking, due to the contraction and expansion of the material under the high temperature changes, which in our climate varies from the cold of winter to the warmth of summer to about 110 degrees Fahrenheit.

Waterproofing

Like all other materials such as stone, brick, marble, etc., cement absorbs more or less moisture. If, however, proper care is taken in the selection of the aggregates and in the proportioning of the mixture, there should be little trouble in obtaining a product that will be sufficiently impervious for all such objects as are described herein, such as concrete pottery and garden furniture. If, however, one wishes to produce an article such as a vase, and desires that it should be absolutely impervious or waterproof, one can make it so by using a waterproofing compound. There are a number of such compounds on the market, all of which have more or less merit. The principle upon which all of these compounds is based is that of filling up the pores or minute holes which are to be found in all materials of a similar nature to that of stone or concrete. These compounds are offered for sale in both powder and liquid form. Some are incorporated in the mixture, and others are used as a surface treatment after the article is complete. The latter class are the simplest to apply, and will answer well for the waterproofing of the articles described in the foregoing chapters.

INDEX

	PAGE
Acid, use of..	101
Air bubbles, how to avoid..............................	30
Alum	75
Amount of ingredients necessary for fixed amount of mixture 104,	105
Antiques, reproduction of........................... 89,	90
Artistic possibilities...................................	1
Assembling fences.......................................	169
Assembling a glue mold...............................	85
Assembling of pedestal.................................	137
Assembling plaster mold.................. 29, 30, 42,	43
Balustrades	173
Baluster, plaster model for....................	175-182
Benches	144
Bench pedestals....................................	149-155
Box for making round molds.......................	36
Caen stones...	103
Carborundum brick...................................	154
Cardboard molds...................................	46-48
Case, plaster.......................... 27, 28, 29,	41
Casting ornaments in sections.....................	130
Casting plaster, method of..........................	23
Clay 21, 34,	48
Clay, covering model with...................... 60,	65
Color pigments..	95
Color, test pieces......................................	95
Colored cements.....................................	89
Colored mortars, preparation of.................	96
Colors, wide range of................................	96
Combination casting and modeling..........	45-58

Index

	PAGE
Combination glue and wood core	87
Combination metal and cement mortar fence	183
Concrete fences	158
Concrete mixtures, preparation of	99
Copings for fences	166
Core, collapsible wood	166
Core, combination cardboard and sand	46-48
Core, piece or sectional	26, 27, 35, 36, 43
Core, plaster	24
Core, solid	25
Concrete pedestals	122
Consistency of mortar	10, 30
Cow's hair	186
Curing cement casts	32
Curing colored cements	98
Cutting out designs	90
Cutting plaster	39
Depositing the cement	30
Designs in colored cement	89
Double tin for melting glues	67
Duplicate pieces	19
Egyptian vase	45
Fences, concrete	158
Fences, foundations for	158
Fence posts	159
Fence post caps	161
Field stone, use of, for fences	107
Finishing coat	11-14
Flexible molds	59
Forming round plaster molds	37-40
Forms, wire	2-9
Foundations for concrete furniture	141
Foundations for fences	158
Frames, wire	2-9
Framework for fence	184
Funnel for glue molds	63-67
Garden furniture	122

Index

	PAGE
Gelatine	67
Glue, best kind to use	66
Glue, double tin for melting	69, 71
Glue, method of preparing	67
Glue molds	59
Glue molds, assembling of	75
Glue molds, method of making simple	59
Glue molds, using old	88
Glue, time required to harden	73
Goat's hair	10
Granite	103
Hand-modeled vase	110
Handles for Egyptian vase	53
Hardening of cement; time required	30
Heavy relief work	59
Importance of water	58
Initial set	108
Inlay work in colors	93-96
Inlaying of tile	113
Joggles	23, 24
Lattice design for fence panel	162
Limestone	103
Low cement copings	170
Marble dust	11
Mineral colors	94, 95
Mixing plaster	22
Models	19, 20, 40
Mold for solid walls	109
Modeling in cement	50
Modeling over wire frames	10
Modeler's clay. (See Clay.)	
Moravian tile	117
Muriatic acid	101
Negative mold	117
Oil	20
Panels, for fences	162
Paper, covering model with	60

Index

	PAGE
Pedestals	122
Plaster, method of mixing	22
Plaster models	39, 40
Plaster molds	19-43
Plaster molds for curved objects	33-44
Plaster mold for square box	20, 31
Plasterer's hair	10
Pointing up	121-136
Portland cement mortar	2-11
Pouring the cement mixture	30
Preparing glue	69
Proportion of aggregates	99
Red granite	103
Reinforcing	55, 124, 132, 134, 150, 153, 164, 167, 182, 189
Removing cast from mold	31
Round core, sectional	35
Rubble fence panel	166
Sand	105-107
Sand, grading of	106
Sectional glue molds	77
Sectional wood mold	128, 129, 131
Selection of aggregates	99
Scratch coat	10-14
Scratch coat for fence	187
Shellac	20
Size of aggregates	101
Slab for bench seat	152
Solid core, method of removing from cast	116
Stones	99
Sundial pedestals	140
Surface finishes	103
Tamping	49
Templates	13, 14, 16, 17, 36, 40, 50, 52
Templates for copings	172, 173
Three-piece outer mold	33, 34
Tile, method of inlaying	117
Time required for cement to set	30

	PAGE
Tin for molds	155
Tools	189
Tooled panels	129
Turning plaster molds	37
Uniform mixing	108
Use for old glue molds	88
Varnish for glue molds	75
Vent holes	65
Voids	105
Wall, solid rubble	168
Washing sand	107
Water, importance of	58
Waterproofing	190
Waterproofing glue mold	74
White marble	103
White Portland cement	94
Wire frames or forms	2-9
Wire lath	3, 5, 6, 8
Wood core, solid	116
Wood model for square box	20
Wood molding, use of	129
Wood, proper kind for molds	147
Wooden molds	110
Working board	20-22

Printed in the United States
100034LV00003B/138/A